JAMES HOWELL

COUNTDOWN TO ATOMGEDDON

THE RACE TO BUILD THE FIRST ATOMIC BOMB

EUROPE

WORKBOOK PRESS LLC
187 E Warm Springs Rd,
Suite B285, Las Vegas, NV 89119, USA

Website: https://workbookpress.com/
Hotline: 1-888-818-4856
Email: admin@workbookpress.com

Ordering Information:
Quantity sales. Special discounts are available on quantity purchases by corporations, associations, and others.
For details, contact the publisher at the address above.

ISBN-13:   978-1-956876-55-0 (Paperback Version)
               978-1-956876-56-7 (Digital Version)

REV. DATE: 30/11/2021

Countdown to Atomgeddon - Europe

The Race to Build the First Atomic Bomb

James Howell

Contents

Acknowledgements

Anne Nelson, *The Red Orchestra*, Random House Publishing Group, New York, NY.

Lt. Lynn Compton, *Call of Duty*, The Berkley Publishing Group, New York, NY.

Robert Edsel with Bret Witter, *The Monuments Men*, Back Bay Books/ Little Brown and Company, New York, NY.

Thomas Powers, *Heisenberg's War*, Alfred A. Knopf, New York, NY.

Elizabeth-Anne Wheal, Stephen Pope & James Taylor, *Encyclopedia of the Second World War*, Castle Books, Secaucus, NJ.

John Cornwell, *Hitler's Scientists*, Penguin Compass, Penguin Group, New York, NY.

Samuel A. Goudsmit, *Alsos*, AIP Press, American Institute of Physics, Woodbury, NY.

Dwight D. Eisenhower, *Crusade of Europe*, Doubleday & Company, Inc., Garden City, New York

General Leslie M. Groves, *Now It Can Be Told*, Da Capo Press, Boston Massachusetts

Michael Dobbs, *Six Months in 1945*, Alfred A. Knopf, New York, NY.

Colonel Boris T. Pash, *The Alsos Mission*, Award Books, New York, NY.

Chapter 1

Blake and Nate Called
Back to Active Duty

It was 0300 hours on August 3, 1944, when Nate and Blake finally arrived at Corpus Christi, Texas. It was dark, hot, and muggy, just the way the Army liked. Both men were called back to active duty after being out of the service for several years. They had been pressed back into active duty to record the results of some foreign mission still unknown. Both men were recruited by the Army at the urging of both the Army CID and the civilian FBI following their involvement in the capture of several conspirators in the desert south of Socorro, New Mexico. They were directly involved in identifying and exposing two physicists working directly with the Manhattan Project in Los Alamos, New Mexico, who were supplying secrets to the Russians. Both men were gifted journalists and would be needed to record and lead teams of scientists charged with the responsibility of helping the allies find needed material and scientists in the race to build the first atomic bomb. Blake had written an article about "heavy water" and another article still unpublished concerning Dr. Werner Heisenberg that had helped persuade Washington and the Army that Germany was in the process of producing a "super bomb" that could destroy a city instead of a single building as current bomb technology was designed. It could be dangerous work. They were to wear military clothing representing the American Army into previously held German-occupied areas. They were also to be prepared to wear civilian clothing as needed to work with various underground groups in Italy, France, and Germany. Nate had also written an article but was unpublished about the "super bomb" His article voiced the concerns that such a bomb would have a devastating effect on innocent civilians as well as the military targets. He had coined the term "atomgeddon" as a combination of atomic energy and the possibility that the bomb could set the world on fire. Currently the technology did not exist to determine what would be the result of such a bomb. The article was not published due to the sensitive nature of the material and the CID had told him not to publish the article for fear of inciting negative public opinion. Secrecy was paramount and the country that developed the "super bomb" could rule the world. Even some of the scientists in the project felt that the detonation of a "super bomb" could set the world on fire and the destruction of all life, thus the moniker "atomgeddon."

The Continental Trailways bus had pulled away from the bus stop at a gas station on the outskirts of Corpus Christi. An olive drab suburban was parked in the shadows waiting for the bus to clear the site before it approached the two men standing by the gas pumps with no baggage. Blake was still half-asleep from the trip while Nate was more alert than a sparrow being stalked by a cat. Nate was first to enter the suburban followed by Blake. "Where are we going?" Blake asked the driver in civilian clothes. The driver responded, "My name is Sergeant Mosher and my orders are to take you to a house on Guthrie Street on the south side of Corpus Christi. That's all I can tell you." Nate was enjoying the secretive nature of the situation and the discomfort that Blake was feeling. As a Navy SEAL, some years back, Nate was well trained and knew what to expect, while for Blake, this was unfamiliar and frightening. Blake preferred to know what was happening and where they were going. Sergeant Mosher was trying to pass the time comfortably with his two passengers and asked, "Where are you from?" "Hope the trip was comfortable." "Have you been to Corpus Christi before?" Apparently about as uncomfortable with the trip as his passengers. Neither of his passengers wanted to talk and just tried to concentrate on the route from the bus stop and to the house. "You will be given your orders in the morning at 0700 hours and don't be late." "Sergeant Smith will show you to your quarters and provide clothing for the briefing in the morning." As they turned on Guthrie Street, a black sedan pulled out of a parking spot along the curb and began following the suburban. Sergeant Mosher tensed and began to watch the rear view mirror. Nate also noticed the black sedan and couldn't help but tell Sergeant Mosher to slow down to let the sedan pass. After slowing to a crawl and the black sedan had not passed, Sergeant Mosher then made a right turn to confirm that the sedan was following them. It was now clear that the suburban was being tailed for some reason. Sergeant Mosher knew what he had to do. He floored the gas pedal and the old suburban began to accelerate. "I'm not sure who or why we are being followed, but should we be separated, call this number and give them the code 'Alsos,'" Sergeant Mosher explained. "Don't contact the local police and take these weapons." Blake was frantic; he had not noticed the trailing sedan until Sergeant Mosher turned the corner and increased his speed. "What's going on?" Blake continued. "I haven't used a weapon in fifteen years." Nate was quick to respond. "Get a little distance between us and the sedan, turn left, and let us out before you continue to try to evade the sedan." "We will wait there for someone to pick us up. Hopefully it will be you." "Okay, make it quick, I'll see you later." Sergeant Mosher pressed on the gas pedal again to gain some space between the two vehicles. "In four blocks, I'll make a left turn, stop, and you guys find a doorway to hide." After making the turn, the suburban rolled quickly to a stop, the passengers exited and found a doorway across the street and out of sight. The sedan made the same turn just as the suburban made another left turn at the end of the block. Sergeant Mosher was still ahead of them, but they were gaining. He had successfully dropped his passengers without notice by the black sedan. He then decided to take the ramp onto Highway 358 and head toward the Corpus Christi Naval Air Station to safety. He reasoned that the black sedan would not attempt to follow him into the Air Station. His speed was higher than the old suburban was designed for and the sedan was getting closer. The black sedan came alongside the suburban at a high rate of speed then pulled into the left rear fender of the suburban. It didn't take much of a hit to cause the suburban to skid uncontrollably and go through the wooden barrier of the bridge over Cayo Del Oso. Fifty feet below, the water of the Cayo Del Oso swallowed the Army vehicle. Sergeant Mosher was within one mile of safety at the Naval Air Station, but the sedan made sure that the suburban and its passengers were not going to make it to safety.

Nate and Blake were still waiting twenty-five minutes later. Without a vehicle or Sergeant Mosher, the prospect of finding the house on Guthrie Street was dismal. Nate figured that they were on the southwest side of Corpus Christi near the Padre

Island Freeway or Highway 358. The area where they had been dropped was an old business district with no residences in sight, and no service stations were visible. "Sergeant Mosher told us to not contact the Corpus Christi police but to call the unlisted number for assistance." "I guess we will have to walk toward the road noise probably from the Padre Island Freeway." "We should be able to find a phone along the freeway." Blake asked, "Do you remember the phone number and code we were given by Sergeant Mosher?" Nate answered, "No, I don't have to remember it. You wrote it down the instant you heard it." Blake was nervous and toying with the weapon that Sergeant Mosher had given him. He kept it concealed in his waistband at his back and covered by a loose-fitting Hawaiian silk shirt. Nate was walking fast and glancing both right and left repeatedly to check for traffic or an opportunity to find a telephone. His weapon was also concealed by the light-colored cotton shirt that was unbuttoned halfway to the waist. As the two men walked in the dark, each block contained the same thing: old business buildings, some still in use but most vacant and none with lights or any sign of life. Many of the street lights were not operating or broken, making their walk more perilous, as they dodged trash and broken concrete sidewalks. Suddenly, Blake heard a vehicle. Nate had also heard the approaching vehicle. As it came closer, it first appeared to be the black sedan that had pursued them before they had jumped out of the military suburban. Nate had ducked into an alleyway and was tugging at Blake's shirt sleeve to follow. The vehicle was approaching very slowly, either looking for something or someone. The driver and passenger both had similar hats. As they came closer, Blake could make out a sign on the side of the black vehicle: "Corpus Christi Police." At first Blake was relieved that they were at least safe from the black sedan that had been chasing them, but he remembered the warning from Sergeant Mosher: "Don't contact the local police." Nate was thinking the same thing and began to move down the alley seeking a hiding spot. There was trash and junk on either side of the alley. Nate took the initiative and dropped to the ground and began pulling the trash, trash cans, and boxes around himself. Blake was slow to respond, but he followed Nate's lead and sat down next to one of the old buildings and began moving trash to conceal his legs and body. The police cruiser had not noticed the two men walking along the sidewalk before they slipped into the alley. The police officer on the passenger side was using their search light to scan the buildings on either side of the street as they passed the alley where Nate and Blake were hiding. The light shone directly on the piles of rubble where the men were but the cruiser continued without slowing or stopping. Just a night patrol checking the safety of the area. Nate was first to stand to begin cleaning the debris from his clothing and Blake followed. It was not as bad as Blake had first imagined; the trash was in big paper bags, cans, and boxes but did not soil his clothing, but the smell was something else. Nate noted,

"That was close, if the police had stopped us with concealed weapons, we would have a lot of explaining to do and probably an overnight stay at the expense of the citizens of Corpus Christi." "It will be light soon and it should be easier to move around to find a phone." Blake finally asked the question that had been bothering him since the black sedan began following them, "Why was that black sedan following us?" Nate responded, "Couldn't be us, unless you have made somebody down here mad like you did in Magdalena, New Mexico." Nate was referring to several attempts on their lives after Blake had stuck his nose into the business of a conspiracy in progress to halt the delivery of military hardware to the Alamogordo Bombing and Gunnery Range. Blake responded, "Couldn't be me. I changed my seven-day deodorant ten days ago and I don't know anyone in this area anyway." "Must have been a case of mistaken identity or maybe Sergeant Mosher was the target of the chase." "Just keep walking. We are bound to find a telephone close to the highway."

The road noise they heard was from the Padre Island Freeway— at least that's what the sign read as they approached the freeway from the north. Not a busy intersection at 0530 hours in the morning, especially since the overhead freeway had cut off an old service station from the traffic, but there was the old service station on the south side of the freeway. There were a few lights from the old service station showing some life and maybe a telephone. Blake finally spoke, "Maybe we can use their telephone, or at least point us in the direction for one." The sun was still below the horizon but the lights were on at the gas station and an attendant was busy putting out a stack of tires and washing down the driveway. Nate was first to ask, "Good morning, sir, may we use your phone?" The attendant was startled at first to see two men walking toward him in the early light. "Can't, the name is Sam and the boss isn't here yet, but give him five minutes and he should show soon." Nate thanked the young man and said they would wait while the attendant continued to wash down the driveway. Nate and Blake were just getting comfortable with their situation and had taken seats on an old couch in front of the service station when another police cruiser exited the freeway and pulled into the service station. The police officer yelled to Sam, "Good morning." Sam just waved and continued to spray water on the driveway. Then the police officer noticed the two men apparently waiting for something or someone. The police officer asked, "Car trouble?" Nate was quick to respond, "No officer, just waiting for someone to pick us up." "He is late and we were looking for a telephone to call him." The officer responded, "I can help you with that. Your wait for the station owner to open may be longer than Sam told you, sometimes even a couple hours." "There is an all-night truck stop about two miles down 358 and I know they have a telephone there." Nate was not anxious to spend any time with the police since they were carrying concealed weapons. Blake, on the other hand, had not considered the weapons and gave a different response. "Great, we appreciate your help." The police officer then said, "No problem, give me a minute to get rid of some coffee and I'll be right back." Nate turned to Blake and asked, "Are you crazy? What if he finds we are carrying firearms? Blake responded, "Maybe we should get rid of them?" Nate responded, "No, we may need them." Before they could decide what to do, the police officer returned and told the two men to get into the cruiser. As they entered the freeway heading south, there were emergency vehicles heading north. The police officer offered, "Had a bad accident this morning." "An Army vehicle crashed through the barrier and fell into the water some fifty feet below." "They have not repaired the highway yet and the traffic is stacking up, seems the driver was killed, an Army sergeant at the Naval Air Station, a Sergeant Mosher." Blake was shocked and beyond speech; they might have been involved in the accident had they not jumped out earlier. Nate was cooler and responded, "Horrible way to go. Do they know what caused the accident?" The police officer added, "No, the vehicle is still in the water and probably will be until they can get a barge from the Naval Air Station with a crane to remove it." The police cruiser pulled off the highway and stopped at the front door of the truck stop. "You guys be careful and have a good day." "There is a telephone just inside the door." Nate responded, "Thanks, officer." He was careful to stand facing the cruiser so that the police officer would not notice the bulge under the back of his shirt.

Blake followed suit and waited until the cruiser was away from the truck stop before he could relax and turn toward the truck stop.

The Black Sedan

"Good work, comrades," the Russian "Mechanic" exclaimed. "You disposed of three of the men that were to be part of the American Alsos teams to take the assets and scientists away from us." "Our agent within the American Alsos headquarters (code-named "Klaus") told us about the forming of the Alsos teams and we are now dismantling these teams, thanks to your work." The driver of the sedan was concerned that the sedan could be identified as the vehicle that pushed the Army vehicle in the water and asked, "What about the sedan? The damaged fender could be traced to the Army vehicle." The "Mechanic" responded, "Not to worry, the sedan will be repaired, repainted, and shipped to Mexico City where it will disappear." "The two journalists from New Mexico have been eliminated along with their driver. Our next task is to find the other members of the Alsos teams for elimination." The driver of the sedan and his associate were then assigned the task of finding the meeting place of the other Alsos members and devise a means to dispose them.

It was late in the afternoon before the two men assigned the task of finding the other members of the Alsos operation began their search. They knew that the safe house was on Guthrie Street, but they did not have the actual address. The street was seventeen blocks long and they would need some good sunlight to be able to identify their targets. As they drove down the street, some of the house numbers were identifiable while most were concealed by overhanging trees and the approaching darkness. The two men decided to wait until morning for more light and a better view of the street and houses. Besides, there were too many people walking their dogs or jogging this time of day who might be able to identify the saboteurs.

The Russians Leave Texas

The two men in the new black sedan began searching for the house on Guthrie Street early the next morning. The light was better, there were fewer people walking in the neighborhood, and the vehicular traffic was nonexistent. They continued down Guthrie Street looking for traces of military vehicles or military personnel. They could find neither. The two men reported back to the "Mechanic" that their search had been without success. The "Mechanic" then explained, "The car you were driving to force the suburban off the highway has been repaired, repainted, and is to be shipped to Mexico tomorrow morning." The "Mechanic" continued, "The Alsos team has moved out of the house and have been flown to London." "We will be moving also." "Our source within the American Alsos headquarters (code-named Klaus) tells us that the two men from New Mexico were not in the Army vehicle as it crashed into the water at Corpus Christi." "They have been flown to London and our new orders are to proceed to Moscow to form three teams similar to the American Alsos teams to recover the assets needed to produce the "super bomb" before the Americans." "We will then intercept the American Alsos teams in their attempts to find the needed assets and Dr. Werner Heisenberg somewhere in Germany." "We have yet to locate Dr. Heisenberg but it is suspected that he may still be in Berlin at the research facility at the Kaiser Wilhelm Institute for Physics." "Klaus, our source within Alsos is very close to determination of Dr. Heisenberg's location and is also reporting that the American Alsos team in Genoa, Italy, is moving north and west toward Marseille, France." "Klaus also reports that the American Alsos teams should have more detailed information by next week and our plans should include finding the shipment of 1,400 tons of uranium ore as it leaves Marseille and moves northward." "Our spies have located a large uranium ore and heavy water supply in a warehouse owned by the Auer Gesellschaft Plant in Oranienbrug which should be safe from the American Alsos teams since it is located deep in our occupational zone." "The Allies have bombed the plant destroying much of the works, but there should be no damage to the uranium we will be seeking." "It would be a breach of the Yalta Accord should the Americans cross into our occupational zone." "Klaus also reports that an American Alsos team is heading south from Paris possibly to intercept the 1,400 tons of uranium ore moving north out of Marseille or the nine railcars headed toward Toulouse or Arles."

The new Russian teams were feeling pushed beyond their capacity. The Americans now had at least three Alsos teams some accompanied by a T-Force pursuing various targets in Germany, Italy, and France. The "Mechanic" finally accepted the fact that they were outmanned and in most cases out maneuvered. Klaus had tried to help by ordering more teams but his efforts had fallen on deaf ears. Most Russian troops and assets were being pushed toward Germany on the Western Front. Klaus finally communicated with the "Mechanic." "You must find a way to complete your missions." "You and I along with your team members will be sent to the Western Front should we fail." He went on to say, "The messages from our handler 'Moscow' was quite clear: complete your missions or die on the Western Front."

The "Mechanic" was awaken abruptly by Sonia to take a radio message from "Moscow." It had been seemingly forever that the darkness had enveloped the train on its way to the

Western Front. Finally, the sun had appeared exposing the long passenger train containing hundreds of Russian soldiers heading to the Western Front and certain death. The "Mechanic" and his teams were on a different mission: they were to find and confiscate valuable assets needed by Russian scientists in order to build a "super bomb." The "Mechanic" had anticipated the message from "Moscow," his contact and handler within the Russian Alsos Group. He also knew that his handler would not be happy. "Moscow" was quick to vent his irritation. "Where are you and when will you find Dr. Werner Heisenberg?" The "Mechanic" responded, "We are two days from Hechingen and Dr. Heisenberg's laboratory and the nuclear reactor." "Moscow" then asked, "Why did you not fly to save time, and why did you need special equipment instead of using the equipment available from regular Russian troops in the field?" The "Mechanic" apologized and allowed "Moscow" to vent the rest of his frustrations before he began his explanation. "There are twelve tons of radioactive uranium ore, uranium bricks used in a very heavy nuclear reactor that must be recovered and moved." "My team will need specialized handling equipment to move the supplies and the reactor." "As soon as we complete the arrangements to move the reactor at Hechingen, we must then drive immediately to Heidelberg and Strasbourg on our way to Hamburg for other equipment and supplies, especially the heavy water in Hamburg." "Moscow" then responded, "Heavy what?" The "Mechanic" wanted to laugh but thought better of it and answered the question. "It is water with small quantities of deuterium in solution or water with an extra hydrogen atom and it is used as a moderator in a nuclear reaction to reduce overheating which could possibly lead to a nuclear explosion." The "Mechanic" continued his explanation, "Our teams must then move to recover the nine railcars of uranium ore in either Toulouse or Arles." "We will be competing with the American Alsos teams at all of these sites and most of our movements will be in British- or American-occupied zones." "The heavy water is most critical to operate the reactor and is stored in the basement of St. Mary's Cathedral in Hamburg." The explanation that the "Mechanic" was offering seemed to mollify "Moscow's" anger and frustration. "Moscow" finally responded, "I don't care what you are doing, just get Dr. Heisenberg before the Americans." "We have the plans, you are gathering the needed materials, now all we need is Dr. Heisenberg to assemble our 'super bomb.'" "Germany is close to developing their own 'super bomb' and I don't want one of them dropped in my bedroom." Dr. Heisenberg must be recovered or you and your team will be spending the rest of the war fighting Germans on the Western Front." "The Alsos teams have been one step ahead of you since your teams were formed." "To catch them and overcome them, it may be necessary to eliminate many of the assets for recovery rather than letting the American Alsos teams find them, but we must have the supplies and Dr.

Heisenberg." "If you can't get ahead of the Alsos teams you may have to leave some of them." "Report back to me if you cannot retrieve one or more of the assets and I will have Special Forces destroy them." The only sound the "Mechanic" heard next was a loud crash of radio microphone being dropped on the floor in disgust."

The "Mechanic" had every right to feel depressed after the call from "Moscow," who had recruited him and his team and now seemed to have abandoned them. He had been their highest and strongest supporter until now and his support was definitely faltering. The possibility of spending the rest of the war fighting Germans on the Western Front would depress anyone, especially since the American Alsos teams were better equipped and well ahead of his teams in gaining the needed assets and Dr. Heisenberg. After several large shots of his favorite vodka, the depression seemed to evaporate. The "Mechanic" then called Sonia to awaken the three team leaders for a conference in his coach. Within fifteen minutes the three team leaders appeared before a very thoughtful "Mechanic." "We have been ordered to hasten our capture of Dr. Heisenberg and some of the assets we were originally assigned to capture." "Dr. Heisenberg, the heavy water and the uranium ore are now our targets of most importance." "Our source of information within the American Alsos headquarters tells us that the Alsos teams are actively seeking the same assets as we have been assigned." "Our original plans were to capture the nine railcars of uranium ore in Toulouse or Arles, but may now be eliminated as a target." "The cyclotron parts and uranium in Strasbourg may remain a secondary target should we finish our work successfully in Hamburg." "It is reported that one of the American Alsos teams will also be operating in the area of the University of Hamburg." "There is also the possibility that the American Alsos team may be accompanied by one of the 'T-Force' commands." Alexei then asked, "What is a T-Force Command?" The "Mechanic" responded, "A specialized team of soldiers trained to protect American Alsos teams that are usually civilians in American Army uniforms and unfamiliar with weapons or combat." "Our source within Alsos tells us that there are approximately 1,500 soldiers now assigned to T-Force Command units and are battle-experienced soldiers and well armed." "Be aware that the T-Forces exist and may be encountered while we challenge the American Alsos teams for the assets needed to produce our super bomb." "Stay in radio contact, speak only in Italian, use your code names, and report any contact with either the American Alsos teams or one of the T-Force teams."

"They must not keep us from accomplishing our goals."

The "Mechanics" Briefings

Team one was to meet the "Mechanic" in his stateroom but he had changed the venue of the meeting to the baggage car. Why he chose to move the meeting was a puzzle to the team but no one argued with him. The "Mechanic" arrived within two minutes of team one to announce, "We are meeting here to examine photographs of your targeted assets." "The first is a store of heavy water and the experimental nuclear reactor or pile moved from Berlin and now located in a cave beneath a high cliff of solid rock in southern Germany." "It is located beneath the former German Kaiser's Castle, Hohenzollern." "Apparently Dr. Heisenberg plays Bach on the organ at the castle in his spare time." "The targets in the area are the two villages of Haigerloch and Hechingen, where both the cave laboratory and Dr. Heisenberg and his associates are located." "According to our source within the American Alsos, the British had placed a British vicar in a church in Hechingen to blueprint the locations of each of the targets and has documented the necessary targets." "The next target is the "atomic machine" or nuclear reactor or "pile" at the Heckingen spinning mill along more of Dr. Heisenberg's associates needed to help assemble our super bomb." "These targets are located in the French occupational zone according to the Yalta Accord but will be pursued by Captain Blake Darnell of one of the American Alsos teams." "Our source indicates that Captain Darnell will not hesitate to cross into the French zone to capture

Dr. Heisenberg and his associates." "It will not deter us from taking Dr. Heisenberg either. He is that important."

The "Mechanic" continued, "We are meeting here in the baggage car to show you the photographs of the area but also to prepare you for the handling of radioactive substances." "You will wear lead-lined gloves, cover your lower body with a lead-lined apron and a Geiger counter which will alert you when high doses of radiation are present." "Dr. Heisenberg's laboratory is located in the two villages of Haigerloch and Hechingen along with the nuclear pile, but it has been reported that he has left Haigerloch by bicycle for his home in Urfeld, about 100 miles from Hechingen." "We will attempt to take the laboratory and the nuclear pile along with any of Dr. Heisenberg's associates that are still located at the laboratory." "We will then proceed to Urfeld to capture Dr. Heisenberg." "There is much to do and little time to accomplish our goals. Continue to study the maps and become familiar with the gear designed to protect you from radiation exposure." "Remember to be especially alert to the American Alsos teams and the French Army in the area." "Continue to study the photographs and get familiar with the safety equipment, it will help keep you alive." "I will leave you now but will return in one hour to finalize your plans of operation." "If you need me in the meantime, I will be with teams two and three."

Teams two and three were studying the aerial photographs of the Hamburg area as the "Mechanic" entered the room. "Comrades, take your seats." "Your team leaders have explained the mission to you and its importance." It will be necessary for you to travel through the French, American, and British zones of occupation and you will have to operate without your Russian uniforms, identification and in civilian clothes as local farmers." "Your team leaders are well equipped to work with the underground as you move from occupational zone to another." "They both speak German and French fluently while they can also speak and understand English." "Each of you have been chosen for your capacity to speak several languages which will be necessary while traveling through the various zone of occupation." "You will have the support of the two underground units operating in the area, the 'Red Orchestra' and the 'White Rose,' both operating in the Hamburg area." "Both underground units are German but are anti-Nazi." "Stay especially alert to German soldiers that are deserters or just lost from their battle groups, but avoid bringing attention to your mission." "You will be traveling in two older farm trucks." "To retrieve the heavy water and the two physicists at the Hamburg University, you must use secondary roads and travel mainly at night to avoid detection by the Allied forces heading toward Berlin." The "Mechanic" continued his instructions with emphasis on the elimination of any American Alsos team they may encounter and especially their team leaders. "Move quickly into Hamburg, find and load the heavy water into the trucks, and proceed to the university to find the two physicists, Drs. Gerlach and Harteck, and their laboratories." "Take anything of value and proceed to Bad Oldesloe where the 'Red Orchestra' underground will have prepared the grass airfield for the landing of a transport to take you to Warsaw, Poland." The "Mechanic" ended his instructions by asking, "Are there any questions?"

Chapter 2

Dr. Otto Smitt Gets the Call

Dr. Otto Smits was grading papers from his analytical chemistry class at New Mexico Institute of Mining and Technology in Socorro, New Mexico, when the phone rang. He picked up the instrument and answered cheerfully. An excited voice said, "Be there at three in the morning!" and the line went dead. Otto was familiar with the voice as a roommate from Hamburg University and a respected colleague, a genius, a doctorate in physics and credentials in several other disciplines. He had asked Otto to get involved in a "project" he was involved in from some unnamed place in the mountains north of Santa Fe, New Mexico. When Otto left Germany in 1940, it was because he was Jewish and feared losing his life and family. He moved to Socorro without knowing where it was but took the first job he was offered. His wife and three kids knew very little English but were anxious to make the change.

Leaving everything they owned in Germany, they paid some Frenchman a lot of money to get them to London and then to New York. The Statue of Liberty was a welcomed site to them. The man who just called him met Dr. Smitt and his family at the harbor in New York, helped them to make arrangements for the trip to New Mexico, and loaned him $2,000 to tide them over until he was meaningfully employed. Otto, of course, was very grateful to his old friend and they had a lot to talk about. They had regular communications over the intervening years, usually sharing scientific theories. The loan had been repaid long ago and his family had visited with his friend in Berkley at the University of California several times.

As Otto drove his 1938 Chevrolet away from Socorro toward the meeting place in Albuquerque, New Mexico, he reflected on his life during the last three years. His work in New Mexico was very different from his work in Germany, but their arrival in Socorro was almost bad enough to make him regret the decision. They had traveled by train from New York to St. Louis then to Albuquerque with very little trouble. The rest of the trip was different. The only train to Socorro was bound for El Paso, Texas, which passed through Socorro and stopped just long enough for Otto and his family to exit. The train was a freight train containing munitions going to Fort Bliss in El Paso, Texas, and really stinky. The AT&SF steam engine belched out mountains of chocking black smoke and there were no passenger cars, making it necessary for Otto and his family to ride in the caboose. The train usually did not stop in Socorro at this time of day, but it made an exception to stop for Otto and his family. They arrived in Socorro at 3:30 in the morning with all their belongings. They were met at the station by a drunk asleep in the waiting room. Otto and his wife managed to get a few intelligible words from him, but no good news. There was no one to meet them, no taxi service, no telephone, no vehicles to rent, just a drunk giving them directions to walk west to downtown Socorro. They gathered their things and started walking toward downtown, dragging most of their baggage. If the moon had been obscured, they would not have made it to the Val Verde Hotel, but by the light of the moon, they made the trip just a mile from the train station, but it was a long trip dragging baggage and Otto's family. The only reception committee were several barking dogs following them to the hotel. By the time they reached the hotel, all employees had either retired to their rooms or gone home, leaving Otto and his family with the only room out of the weather. It was the heavy leather furniture in the lobby but a welcomed place to rest for the night. It wasn't the best reception, but Otto and his family was just glad to have completed their journey.

The call Otto had received from his friend directed him to a location in Albuquerque where the two men could discuss the "project." Otto's abilities and education were of great importance to the "project" his friend was explaining. "Three languages, analytical chemistry, doctoral student of Dr. Werner Heisenberg in theoretical physics, makes you particularly important to the 'project' and I want you to return to Europe." "I want you to be part of the 'project' called 'Operation Alsos' under the direction of top Washington War Department personnel."

Nate and Blake: The Unlisted Telephone Number

"I can't believe Sergeant Mosher is dead," Nate noted. "I wonder if we were supposed to be in the car with him when it went off the bridge, and if the black sedan was involved." Blake responded, "Probably just an accident. I can't believe someone would intentionally push an Army vehicle off the bridge." Nate was still considering whether they were supposed to be in the vehicle with Sergeant Mosher. "What are we getting ourselves into? I thought we were supposed to just record a mission in Europe and not be in any danger." Blake finally said, "One of those imponderables that we shouldn't ponder over." "Let's get to the phone and call for help and get some food before I collapse from hunger." Nate agreed. "Great, you call while I try to get the garbage stench off my beautiful Hawaiian shirt." By the time Nate finished his cleaning job, Blake had called the unlisted number and they were sending a civilian vehicle to pick up the two men. It was Blake's turn to tidy up and Nate was going to place a quick to-go order for two tin foil–wrapped ham sandwiches. "Two bags of potato chips to add to that order," Nate explained. A few minutes later a black Ford coupe stopped in front of the restaurant.

The driver of the '35 Ford coupe came in the restaurant door looking for the two men to be taken to the house on Guthrie Street. The driver was another sergeant in uniform with a name tag of Smith. Nate was watching for him and recognized the name of the person to assist them at the house on Guthrie and approached with his hand out. "You looking for a couple of journalists to take to Guthrie Street?" The sergeant responded, "Keep your voice down. You may be in danger." "Let's get going." Nate had to say, "We need to wait for Blake. He went to the restroom but should be back any minute." The soldier told Nate to wait for Blake while he waited in the car at the curb. Blake appeared momentarily and as he came up to Nate, he was cleaner and definitely smelled better. Nate said, "Let's go. Our driver is out front waiting for us. I got shotgun, you have to sit in the back." Blake didn't care where he sat as long as he had a sandwich. "Where are my potato chips?" Blake asked.

The trip to the Guthrie Street house was smooth and uneventful. Blake and Nate finished their sandwiches while Sergeant Smith drove. Blake finally asked, "What happened to Sergeant Mosher? Was it an accident?" The sergeant responded, "We don't know yet. The barge with the crane should be pulling the vehicle out of water very soon, but we suspect that it was an accident." Nate didn't bother explaining what had happened to them while traveling with Sergeant Mosher and why they had not been taken to the house on Guthrie. He knew he would eventually need to tell someone, but he wanted to wait until the vehicle had been recovered and they could meet with the authorities. Blake was feeling the same without mentioning anything to either the driver or Nate. They would also have to explain how they were given the weapons still in their waistbands. Sergeant Smith pulled into the driveway midway down the 2300 block of Guthrie Street. The sergeant parked the car under a carport designed for two cars and walked quickly to the back door where another soldier was seated just inside the door sporting one of the new M1 rifles. Nate had heard about the weapon introduced in 1936 but had not seen one. As a retired Navy SEAL, Nate was familiar with many of the weapons in use and planned by the armed forces and wanted to take a look at the weapon. Nate asked the soldier, "May I take a look at your weapon?" Sergeant Smith quickly interrupted Nate and explained that the soldier was not to share his weapon with anyone and he was there for their protection. "He is standing guard duty to make sure no harm comes to you." "Let's get you guys settled in and show you what you will be wearing tomorrow for the briefing." "Major Powers will explain your mission along with two other men." Blake asked the question this time, "What have we gotten ourselves into?" Nate didn't respond but was as concerned as Blake, but he wasn't going to show it—he was an ex-Navy SEAL and had to display superhuman strength and fortitude, whether he wanted to or not. Blake asked, "What should we do with the weapons we were given by Sergeant Mosher? I really feel uncomfortable concealing them around these soldiers." As Blake was asking the question, Sergeant Smith entered their room and couldn't help but hear Blake's question. The sergeant responded, "If you were given weapons by Sergeant Mosher you should keep them but keep them on safe and out of sight. Sounds like you did meet Sergeant Mosher." "You can explain it to me later." The sergeant had brought clothing for the two men and had asked them to test them before the briefing. Sizing would be the issue since both men had been out of the service several years and their bodies had changed, maybe a little drooping and expanding here and there. Sergeant Smith watched as the two men tried on their new military attire. Nothing out of the ordinary, just Army issue fatigues, boots, and fatigue caps. Everything fit satisfactorily, very loose. The interesting thing about the uniform was the lack of identification. There was none—no name patch, no rank insignia or stripes, and no unit designation. Just plain Army issue fatigues. Nate asked, "Will we be issued ID tags?" The sergeant's answer was not reassuring. "No, you will not be identifiable, no point in asking any other questions, save them for the briefing tomorrow." Nate had to ask one more question, "Can we have holsters for these weapons or just stick them in our pants' pockets?" The question was answered by the sergeant handing both men a holster for their weapons. Then the sergeant ordered, "Now take a shower, get that stink off, lunch is in the refrigerator, play some cards or pool or just read but be ready for breakfast at 0600 hours, the briefing is at 0700 hours."

The Briefing

Neither man slept much. Blake was trying to figure how he got involved in this situation and Nate was just excited by the suspense and the secretive nature of the assignment. Nate could remember the feeling from each SEAL mission, not knowing what they were doing and to whom or where they were going, but somehow the leaders found a way to complete each mission without losing precious personnel. Blake's Army service was in personnel as a clerk typist and there were no missions and there were very few times that he was required to fire a weapon just to retain his proficiency and pay grade. This was an unfamiliar war to Blake—his service was keeping records intact of new and departing personnel. His war was with multiple onion-skin copies, carbon copies, and erasers. His armament was his typewriter. Apparently that was about to change.

At 0600 hours Nate was up and dressed before Sergeant Smith opened the door to announce breakfast. Blake had finally fallen asleep after many hours of heavy thinking. Nate pulled the covers off him and threw his new clothing onto his face. "Get dressed, breakfast is served." Reluctantly, Blake began to dress but wished for more sleep. "What time is it?" Blake asked. Nate flashed a big grin and said, "It's breakfast time, but you can go back to sleep if you like. I'll eat your breakfast for you." Neither of the men had time to brush their teeth or wash their faces, when Sergeant Smith reappeared and told them that breakfast will end in fifteen minutes. Even Nate was having trouble readjusting to the tight Army schedule but decided he may as well get used to it and left for the kitchen without waiting for Blake. Still feeling sleepy, Blake reasoned that he could brush his hair and comb his teeth after breakfast, but looks like shaving would be out of the question.

There were two other men seated at the table when Nate arrived. He introduced himself and was about to dish out some eggs when Blake arrived and did the same. The other two men were also civilians recently inducted again for an unspecified reason and time. "My name is Dr. Otto Smitt and this is Dr. Reginald Graff." Sergeant Smith interrupted the introductions, "No personal information will be discussed beyond your name and where you are from." "No telephone numbers, addresses, rank, blood type, or girlfriends will be discussed." "You are better off not knowing anything about the guy next to you." "More instructions will be made available to each of you at the briefing." As promised, the food on the table disappeared very quickly, forcing everyone to eat fast, if they wanted anything. The other two men appeared much like Blake and Nate: just out of bed without much sleep. Sergeant Smith gave each man several pieces of paper to read before the briefing. He told them to read the information carefully, sign them, and return them to the briefing. Apparently some kind of disclaimer and notice of secrecy and something about duty to your country and another item about life in prison or being shot. The briefing was to be held in the room down the hall. That being said, Sergeant Smith joined the other soldier at the back door and ignored the four men at the table.

By 0645 Nate had finished reading his literature twice and Blake was close behind. The forms were signed and taken by Sergeant Smith. It was time to find out what was to happen to them. Since both Nate and Blake had been reporters for the *Mountain Mail* in Magdalena, New Mexico, reading had been easy for them and retention was usually pretty good. They were both good at manipulating words to make them fit an idea or a space in a sentence. As they moved from their room to the briefing room, an Army staff car was delivering a gentleman in civilian clothes. He went directly to the briefing room without speaking to either the soldier on guard at the door or Sergeant Smith. The man in civilian clothes finally spoke, "Gentlemen, take a seat, make yourself comfortable, and smoke if you have them." "My name is Major Powers." "I will be your mother, brother, girlfriend, and boss while you are on duty and you will address me as Powers in the future while communicating by any means except person to person. Each of you will have code names when talking to others to be used for the same purpose and you will have various ranks. This will not be a dictatorship but a democracy with each of us at equal rank. That will change as needed, but to stay out of trouble, do as you are told." The briefing continued for two hours where details of their assignments were discussed. "The jumping-off place is here." "You cannot discuss what you are doing, where you are going, with anyone." "From now on we will be a team with one mission: to commandeer as much raw material as possible, to capture as many scientists and physicists as possible, and either capture or destroy the laboratories of German scientists so that they do not fall into the hands of Russians." "We will be at war with the Germans, Russians, and the French underground to acquire needed materials for the United States in the race to build the first atomic bomb." Sergeant Smith came into the room and interrupted Major Powers. The two men were discussing something very quietly and apparently very important. "Gentlemen, we have learned that one of our drivers was killed yesterday and it appears that his vehicle was forced off the bridge." "It appears to be sabotage." "We think our mission has been compromised and it is imperative that we leave Corpus Christi tonight." "Sergeant Smith will now explain where we will be going and how we will get there." "Good day gentlemen. See you this evening."

Blake thought the time had come that they tell Sergeant Smith about the black sedan that was tailing them and Sergeant Mosher and how they had escaped before his car was forced off the bridge and into the water. The sergeant responded, "It's probably too late for us to do anything here, but I will pass the information on to CID." "The sedan has probably disappeared by now." "The damage has been done, and we are lucky that your two were not involved in the accident."

At 0400 hours, the Lockheed A-29 Hudson aircraft from the Corpus Christi Naval Air Station was taxing along the tarmac at RAF Mindenhall. It was dark and quiet when the five men left the airfield for the London safe house. The airfield was located about ten miles northeast of Cambridge but a long drive to the London safe house. Nate and Blake were feeling the time difference and the flight was long and noisy. The big transport was efficient but uncomfortable. Although the men leaving the aircraft knew what their new mission was, each of them was introspective about their roles and whether they would be capable of performing their assigned duties. Powers tried to help the men relax unsuccessfully. He was thinking along the same lines as the other men, but his CID experience had taught him to keep his feelings to himself and he was relying on Nate as a Navy SEAL to help do the same with the other men.

It was still dark when the two 1938 Humber Super Snipe vehicles pulled into the underground garage at the safe house in central London. The three-story concrete and brick building had just received the two vehicles in the basement garage as the door magically closed behind them. There was space for several vehicles but from the street, the house appeared to be a normal three-story flat. MI6, the military branch of British Intelligence, and the CID were prepared to receive the small group of men as they arrived from the United States. Each man had been given their orders and been briefed as to their mission upon landing at their respective locations. Nate was to head a team headed for Denmark while Blake was to follow the landing at Normandy and work his way toward Paris.

Time was of the essence. Blake was to leave immediately for South Hampton to board a battle cruiser headed to an unnamed beach at Normandy, France. It was the largest known deployment of man and material to make an amphibious invasion to push the Germans out of France. By July 1944, there were 1,332,000 military personnel involved in the D-Day landing. Casualties were high on both sides of the invasion with 120,000 Allied troops killed and 113,059 casualties on the

German side of the conflict. The news of the initial landing force was costly in human life but had succeeded in routing the Germans at the beach and Blake's ship was to deliver him and another one thousand troops to continue the Allied push toward Paris. As the cruiser neared "Sword Beach," where Blake and the one thousand additional troops were to be deposited, the scene on the beach was amazing. The landing crafts were delivering fresh troops and material by the hundreds. Tanks, trucks, and vehicles of all descriptions were visible marching up the beach just behind the advancing troops.

Chapter 3

Blake Lands at Normandy

Blake's first assignment following his miraculous rise in rank to Capt. Blake Darnell was the "Sword Beach" at Normandy. As noted in the briefings, rank would change as needed and Blake now needed to be a military officer and gentleman. It was almost embarrassing to follow the troops onto the bluff over "Sword Beach" that day. It was June 6 and it had been a roaring success but Allied losses were obvious. The process of gathering bodies from the awful beach area looked like a nightmarish job. The graves registration men were having a hard time containing their emotions and eating their breakfasts. Some couldn't, as one of them spoke to Blake as he passed. "I am just grateful that I came ashore alive and in one piece. These guys were not as lucky." "So many wounded and dead." "They deserve to be honorably identified and buried with dignity as the heroes they are." The grave registration soldier was a corporal and Blake couldn't help but notice that the soldier was gushing with tears as he spoke. He continued his morbid job as Blake came up to his side and hugged him by the shoulder. In the Army, you are taught to be more stoic and it is almost criminal to display emotion and especially for a captain to hug a corporal but the gesture was needed by both men.

The invasion was a success but Blake couldn't help thinking that the cost was too great. He felt guilty that his landing was so easy and added an admiring salute to the corporal as he went about his duty of identifying soldiers. The corporal returned the salute as Blake left the beach.

Blake moved up the beach to an official looking tent on a bluff overlooking "Sword Beach" and presented his orders to the British colonel in command. The colonel seemed surprised at his orders but ordered an American Army driver and jeep to take the captain anywhere he wanted to go and the orders were signed by the Secretary of War. The British colonel handed Blake his papers and noted, "Don't see many of you blokes with papers like that."

There was still some sporadic small-arms fire close by as he headed away from the beach and the distant thunder of artillery. Blake continued up the beach to the assigned jeep and driver. As Blake approached the jeep, he saluted the PFC that had come to attention and saluted. Blake did a double take at the M1 rifle the PFC driver was holding. "Do I get one of those?" The driver handed him his new M1 weapon and asked, "Are you carrying the officer's assigned .45 Colt pistol?" Blake answered in the affirmative before taking the seat next to the new driver. Blake then asked, "What is your name and where are you from?" The new driver answered, "My name is Private First Class Juan Martinez from El Paso, Texas." "I was drafted while attending Texas Western College due to too much parting and not enough studying." It was a nice surprise that PFC Martinez had studied French for two semesters along with his business coursework. He was very good with the road signs and could communicate with just about perfect French. Martinez had been a tank crewman until it was lost in the surf off one of the beaches then assigned to a motor pool as a driver by some brilliant soul in the first personnel section that he stumbled into. (Blake cringed at the thought of how screwed up the Army could be.) Blake's new rank and jeep allowed him and PFC Martinez to move toward Paris without delay. It was dangerous, with both infrequent German small-arms fire from retreating German troops and the Allied traffic moving toward the battle line. There was little that Blake could accomplish outside of Paris other than plan how to accomplish his assigned mission, "Operation Cellastic." Martinez finally asked, "Where to, boss?" To which Blake answered, "There is nothing we can do until we reach Caen which is being attacked by British forces under Field Marshal Montgomery." "We will follow them into Caen as it is liberated." "It may take a while but reports indicate the city may be liberated at any time." Martinez than asked, "What are we supposed to do until the British liberate Caen?" Blake answered, "You know how to play wisk or poker?" "I know it's a horrible way to fight a war, but if we get too impatient, we may get shot." Martinez was really confused now. "What are we supposed to be doing that we have to wait for the British to liberate Caen?" Blake felt that Martinez deserved an explanation about Operation Cellastic, but there was little he could explain without disclosing secret information. When Blake finally explained some of the details of what he was doing, Martinez wanted to help. Captain Darnell explained, "You're going to help me find a few French scientists who could be a threat to our country's efforts to win the war, and we don't want them to fall into the hands of the Russians." We will be moving just behind the advancing Allied forces until we reach Paris where we will be stationed for some time." "It is imperative that you tell no one where you are going or doing." Martinez reluctantly agreed and thus became the first of Blake's Alsos team members as they waited for the other team members and the advance of the Allied forces to clear their way to Paris.

Martinez was helpful in other respects too. He magically "found" things that Blake needed, including maps and food—

even some very nice French cheese, bread, and wine. Blake finally dropped the rank issue and told Martinez that he was a civilian sent to do a job and that in the future he should be called Blake. The guilt Blake felt at the ease of his landing at "Sword Beach" was returning as the two men shared a simple picnic of cheese and wine about a mile behind an American artillery unit blazing away at defending German forces. Blake finally broke the silence between the two men, thinking of their landing and just thankful to be alive. "We need to find a way around the American force and stay close to the British as they move toward Caen." "We also need to find a place to stay while we wait on the British. Any suggestions?" Martinez responded, "You dumbass 'Gringo,' you're going to get us killed." "I have a better idea. Let's go back to the beach and get some help, like a tank battalion!" Blake was shocked at the response from Martinez, but he was right. It was dangerous this close to the battle lines. Besides, the Allied traffic and occasional rifle fire there had been several German planes strafing the area. Martinez had avoided being hit by hiding in the shade of the nearest tree. But, as they moved along a dirt road with no overhanging trees for cover, a German ME109 strafed the area with its guns blazing and shot out the windshield of their jeep. "Our luck is still holding." Blake finally responded in an apologetic squeaky voice, "Perhaps you are right. Let's wait for a little help." "Let's stay put and wait for the fighting to move out of our area. Pass the cheese and wine."

About an hour later, a passing military police unit found Blake and Martinez asleep under a tree along the dirt road. The sergeant leading the MP prodded the two men awake. "How can you guys sleep with all this noise of the battle around you?" Martinez answered, "No problem, we have nothing better to do." The sergeant then asked if they were wounded or just wasting time. Blake finally explained their purpose in "wasting" time. "We have to wait until the British have liberated Caen and follow them into the city." "In the meantime, why don't you and your MPs join us in a wonderful meal of some really tasty K-rations?" Martinez felt it was a rude awakening and hard to explain to the MPs but they did have a nice breakfast with them: cheese, wine, and America's finest K-rations. Following their meal with the military police unit, Blake and Martinez knew the fun was over. Martinez knew that the Germans would be shooting back at the Allied Artillery just in front of them and the stray artillery shell might end their rest period. Not to mention the infrequent German ME109 that might return at any time. The two men decided to sit tight until some help could arrive. They agreed that "patience is a virtue" and may keep them alive. When Martinez and Blake finally did begin to move, they followed a British tank battalion that passed by the next day. The only problem was that they couldn't see more than twenty feet ahead due to the dust and rocks churned up by the tank tracks. It was so bad that their jeep suffered a crushed front end from running into the back of one of the tanks when it suddenly stopped. The tank commander was really upset that his tank had received some small scratches—figure that. They also found that traveling with a tank battalion wasn't the safest either. Sporadic fire from snipers, a stray artillery shell shot over the battle line, a bazooka shell fired by a retreating German soldier, and the dust made for uncomfortable travel. Finally they decided to get off the road and find some shelter behind the advancing British troops. Blake reported his slow progress toward Paris to Alsos headquarters, received very little sympathy, but had received instructions to be patient. Finally, on the morning of the third day of waiting, Martinez came across a partially burned farmhouse where they were more comfortable waiting. Blake had been told that a T-Forces Command team of six soldiers would find them and proceed to Caen with them. The advance toward Paris was very slow, and the small T-Force team would accompany Blake to Paris following the liberation of Caen. Blake was to become attached to one of the T-Force teams for safety until they reached Paris.

It was much more of an adventure now that they were on their own not knowing where they were, no tank or T-Force team to protect them. The two men were becoming attached to their burned-out farmhouse. Corporal Martinez finally found a friendly farmer who advised them the name of a nearby town which they found on their map, exactly where they wanted to be, on the road to Caen. Unfortunately, the city had not been cleared of enemy activity and they would have to wait for further orders and the promised T-Force team. That meant more nights in the old farmhouse and more K-rations. The British forces finally captured Caen on June 24, or eighteen days since their landing at Normandy. Blake, Martinez, and the small T-Force team made themselves comfortable in another burned building in Caen and replenished their supply of K-rations and also some of the C-rations they had been without for some ten days. It would be a long wait to enter Paris, which was finally liberated on August 25. It was a waiting game, but as a result, the Germans surrendered the city without a serious battle which would have caused serious damage to the "City of Lights."

While Blake's team waited to move to Paris, it was learned that some of the uranium shipped from Belgium bound for Toulouse had been moved to Bordeaux. Major Powers ordered Blake to recover the uranium in Bordeaux. "And confiscate some good wine while you are there." Blake questioned the wisdom of this order since much of the area between Casen and Bordeaux was occupied by the Germans. Major Powers was not amused. "I guess you have not heard that the German forces have lost their will to fight since being encircled by Allied forces." "During the first three weeks of April, the Allies had captured over one million German prisoners between Caen and

Bordeaux." "Now get your butt in gear and find the uranium in Bordeaux."

Blake decided it was time to get some help from the French Underground Army (FFI). His contact was a Frenchman named Adnet who lived in the village of Bloye on the Garonne River near Bordeaux. Blake's team was now complete with the addition of the four T-Force members and the two physicists from Los Alamos, James Roemer and Brian Jenkins. Martinez and Roemer both spoke French fluently and volunteered to contact the Frenchman and would ask for his assistance in finding the uranium supposedly moved to Bordeaux from Toulouse. The only information they had was the numbers of the nine railcars as they left Belgium bound for Toulouse.

The Bordeaux Uranium Railcars

The small outdoor café was quiet where Martinez and Roemer were to contact Adnet. The waiter took their order and felt a small piece of paper being pushed into his hand by Martinez. The waiter immediately retreated into the kitchen to read the message and called Adnet as directed by the note. It was unusual for two American soldiers to be leisurely drinking coffee in the café especially with the continued threat of German deserters or loyal troops left behind during the recent resignation of most of the German troops in the area. The waiter then asked the two soldiers to follow him into the kitchen for more privacy. "Adnet will be at this address and make sure you are not followed." The two American soldiers thanked the waiter, paid for their coffee, and slipped out the back door of the café to find Adnet.

Adnet was surprised to hear from the American soldiers. "We have ended our fighting with the Germans since most have been captured or retreated." Martinez was quick to correct the misunderstanding that Adnet had thought he would be asked to participate in action against German troops. "We are not a combat team. We just seek information about some railcars from Belgium." "The railcars contained vital material to help the Allies end the war and we need you to help either locate the railcars or determine what happened to them." "It should not be dangerous but the area is basically off limits to us and in the custody of French and British troops." Adnet was thinking about the request and finally explained, "The Port of Bordeaux is basically cordoned off from all traffic due to the possibility of booby traps throughout the port set by retreating German troops." "The information you seek may be outside the cordoned off area, but even if it is in the restricted area, we should be able to access to the area." Martinez then gave Adnet the railcar numbers and described the contents are barrels of "yellow dirt" but dangerous to handle. Adnet took the information and instructed the two Americans to meet him back at his home at midnight.

Martinez and Roemer returned to the café for some lunch and more of their great coffee. It would be several hours before they were to meet with Adnet and had nothing else to do.

Adnet had found the information that the Americans requested. He was surprised at the ease of finding the railcars located on a siding beside a large warehouse. Of the nine railcar numbers given to Adnet, only two could be identified. Unfortunately the railcars were empty. The information came from one of the secretaries in the rail yard. The contents of the railcars were off-loaded onto several German trucks, taken to the port with a final destination somewhere in Japan. The secretary said the name of the Japanese town was not pronounceable but the route of the shipment went around the Cape of Good Hope. The secretary also indicated the shipment left port several months earlier with a shipping code of U-235—unusual number unless it was a submarine. She continued to explain that the shipment may have been part of the lend-lease program between Germany and Japan.

Adnet met the two Americans at the appointed time. "I think I have found your railcars of 'yellow dirt.'" "My source gave me the information quickly and easily as if someone had asked for the same information recently." "It is possible that either the British or the Russians had also asked for the same information of the secretary." "There were two railcars, but were empty." "The only trace of the 'yellow dirt' was a billing showing that the shipment was off-loaded by the Germans and shipped to Japan." Martinez and Roemer were disappointed but pleased that the shipment did not end in the hands of the Russians. "We really appreciate your help finding the railcars. Is there anything we can do for you in return?" Adnet was glad to help but needed nothing now or the immediate future in support of the underground. "You are welcome and I hope the information you received will help end the war."

Martinez and Roemer reported the information to Blake before taking a break to find something to eat and grab a quick nap. Martinez then asked, "Any progress toward Paris?"

Paris was finally liberated by French troops led by General LeClerc at 8:55 the morning of August 25. It was a long wait for Blake and his team but they finally succeeded in following the French troops into Paris.

Operation Cellastic

Blake's first assignment was Operation Cellastic, which was to gain access to Paris as soon as German forces were driven out of the area. His assignment to find the railcars in Bordeaux was not expected. He could not follow the Allies into Paris as the area was cleared of German troops.

It was the College de France where famed French nuclear physicist Dr. Joliot-Curie maintained his laboratory. The fighting in and around Paris was still active but was generally limited to small-arms fire, but Blake and Martinez decided to try to infiltrate while the fighting continued around them. The streets were virtually clear of debris. There was small-arms fire between advancing and departing forces while snipers kept them alert at all times. The Germans had occupied Dr. Joliot-Curie's laboratory for some time but had left it to operate independently in France due to the size and weight of much of the equipment. The German scientists had used it for several years without moving it to Germany. The college was the location of one of the only working cyclotrons in Europe, which was very heavy and valuable, while the Americans had twenty of the devices in operation. The college had suffered damage, but none was noted to the equipment at the laboratory and still very usable. The laboratory personnel had helped the French underground occasionally by building "Molotov cocktails" to be used against German forces as they retreated, in addition to their normal work with the cyclotron. Dr. Joliot-Curie had been wrongfully identified as being a communist sympathizer and at first identified as not needed by the Allies for interrogation on his research for fear that the Russians would get any information gained immediately following any questioning. The maintenance people at the university were helpful in identifying the two men responsible for running the laboratory and the location of other assets around Paris. Dr. Joliot-Curie had moved to his home away from the university. Blake at first decided that he would not require Dr. Joliot-Curie to accompany them until he reported the situation to Alsos headquarters. Major Powers disagreed and quickly issued orders that Dr. Joliot-Curie should be flown to London for questioning along with his research papers and as much equipment as possible. Blake had his hand slapped sufficiently and arranged to locate the doctor and have him moved to an airfield where Dr. Joliot-Curie was flown to London to meet with Major Powers. One of the engineers that Dr. Joliot-Curie had identified as one of the men that ran the cyclotron in the laboratory was code-named "Cleo." Martinez had located him by asking one of the ground maintenance personnel at the university. He responded, "No, I know no Cleo." Martinez then produced a recent photograph found in the laboratory on the bulletin board. He then responded, "Oh, of course, that is 'Bothe,' a young engineer from Strasbourg, you can find him at the cantina 'Lilli' there," as he pointed to an outdoor cantina across the street from the university. Martinez thanked the man and headed for the cantina. He had found the engineer but was concerned that his confronting the young engineer might cause him to flee before Blake could question him. Blake was nearby and Martinez decided to contact him for assistance and direction before contacting the engineer. Blake was searching the five-story corporate building of Auer Chemical Company, a producer of uranium metal and thorium, when Martinez approached and asked, "I've found one of the engineers that ran the cyclotron in Dr. Joliot-Curie's laboratory." Blake was ecstatic. "Where is he? That's really good news. Can we approach him now?" Martinez explained the situation and waited for Blake to respond. "Let's go find him, but just get acquainted and do not question him yet about the cyclotron." "Just let him know of our interest in Dr. Joliot-Curie and where we might find his research papers." Blake was not participating in the conversation since he did not speak French, but he could tell that Martinez and the engineer were having a cordial conversation. He didn't care what it was about, as long as the engineer spoke freely and trusted Martinez. The conversation was even more cordial as some lovely girls pedaled their bicycles by the cantina. The engineer and Martinez seemed to be admiring all the outstanding parts of the girls but concentrated on their breasts. Martinez and the engineer would giggled and then explain to Blake what they were doing. Just having fun. The engineer wanted to have some fun at Blake's expense and whispered something to Martinez. Martinez grinned and then mentioned to Blake, "Check out that rack." Blake turned, expecting to find a particularly gifted young lady. To his surprise, the only thing visible from his vantage point was a large elk's head with a massive set of antlers. "Very funny!" Martinez and the engineer burst out laughing while Blake could only turn various shades of embarrassment; besides, he did not how to laugh in French. Another couple of drinks and a meal on Major Powers's budget led the conversation to more serious matters. Martinez had asked the engineer about Dr. JoliotCurie and his cyclotron. The engineer volunteered the doctor's address where he had retreated with his research work as most of the Germans left Paris. He also volunteered the names of the two physicists that worked with the cyclotron. Without waiting for a response, he continued, "They have moved much of the laboratory and their research material to the laboratory in Strasbourg, they did not want to find themselves in the custody of the French following the German occupation." "The cyclotron should still be in the laboratory. It's too heavy to move." "The operators of the cyclotron would be considered German sympathizers and possibly shot or publicly ridiculed and their reputations would be ruined." Blake was pleased with the information and thanked the engineer. He would not be needed for more questioning and should be safe staying with the laboratory and not publicly considered a German sympathizer.

Blake and Martinez were amazed how easily they traveled in the city. Although they were told by military police to stay away from the college, they told the MPs that their mission required them to approach the college and that they would need their help in moving the equipment in the laboratory. Of course, the MPs thought that was a really dumb idea and told them to take the issue to Sergeant Blazer, the NCO in charge of the MPs. After Sergeant Blazer listened to Blake and read his orders, signed by the War Department, he said he would help where possible. The major piece of equipment the allies wanted and did not want the Russians to have was the cyclotron that Dr. Joliot-Curie had built and had maintained during the German occupation. The cyclotron was not a light piece of equipment and would require a large truck to haul it and a lift or possibly a crane to remove the unit from the college. No easy chore to gather this needed equipment during active fighting. Martinez had been promoted by Blake to sergeant to eliminate much of the bickering between personnel working on details for the move of the equipment. Martinez was promoted to sergeant, at least temporarily. Blake had "borrowed" sergeant's stripes from the Allied headquarters and the required paperwork was not completed. Most military personnel would not respond to the orders from a corporal, but a sergeant had some authority. Now that Martinez had been promoted he had the power to act and speak with authority, just like he wanted. His persona and hat size had doubled. Martinez and Blake had a new job: moving the heavy cyclotron back to the beaches of Normandy for transport to England. Major Powers told the teams that rank would be changed as the situations dictated and Blake felt this situation made it necessary that Martinez be given the rank of sergeant.

With the help of several MPs and the T-Force personnel, the cyclotron was loaded into one of the trucks and left Paris for the trip back to the beach at Normandy to be loaded onto a cargo ship headed to the United States.

Chapter 4

Nate Gets a Promotion

Well, not exactly. Nate was to help open the next area of operation for Alsos. It was to be opened in the area north of Germany and the new commander of the northern effort was Major Brownfield. Nate's new position was lieutenant, driver, and protector for Drs. Smitt and Graff, the physicists assigned to the northern Alsos operation and leader of the Alsos team headed to Hamburg. There were two actual active military personnel also assigned to the team to land at Arhus, Denmark, to establish a headquarters in a large warehouse on the southeastern coast. The group was told that the need for a warehouse was to store and to ship equipment and supplies to the United States as it was received from the various operations in and around Germany. That was about all they were told.

Nate's new code name was not to his liking—"Smitty"—due

to the fact that every time someone called for Dr. Smitt, or Smitty, they both responded. Finally, Dr. Smitt claimed the code name he was to be addressed as "Black" with no reference to his title. Dr. Graff made a similar decision to be called "Clark," again with no reference to his actual title. The military personnel in the group remained with their actual names and name tags, but any indication of rank was missing. There were two military personnel that were not NCOs; they were officers and their ranks were never disclosed. They were "captains" but were actually civilian physicists. The rest of the military personnel in the group were two sergeants. The group was told that the code names and lack of rank was for their protection and that they would be assigned tasks without any knowledge of its importance or function. Supposedly for their protection should they be captured and questioned by the enemy. More likely to protect the Alsos mission. If they were captured and didn't know anything, they could not divulge any critical information. Each member of the team was issued new orders and papers signed by the War Department before each mission and given instructions to whoever read them to help the person presenting the papers at all costs. The group was flown into Naval Station, Arhus, in southeastern Denmark, on April 5. They arrived at 2100 hours to be conveyed by bus to a large hangar on the grounds of the naval air station. Brownfield led the way for the small group into the cavernous interior of the hangar to point out the areas for their lodgings. The group proceeded into a large office in the rear of the hangar, to the dismay of everyone. It had no windows, no source of heating, poor lighting, and just cubicles with six-foot-tall walls with a bed, one nightstand, a chair, and a footlocker for their clothing. Nate had to ask, "Where is my door and where are the bathrooms?" Brownfield explained, "The head is over there in the corner. Don't worry, you won't be here very long. Breakfast will be at 0500 and briefing at 0600, now get some sleep, you leave for your first mission tomorrow morning." Most members of the team dispersed to their cubicles or sat in small groups discussing their situations. The two physicists were busy with chalk and chalkboard playing something that looked to Nate like tic-tac-toe but with unknown characters and without a winner or a loser, just "techese."

At the 0600 briefing, the group learned that their mission was to capture the centrifuge at the University of Hamburg and any research material pertaining to its operation. The centrifuge is the reason for the needed space at Arhus Naval Station where there will be more items to store before shipping to London. This will be our staging area until we can move closer to Berlin. Nate had been issued an American jeep and a new Army M1 rifle and a Browning automatic .45 caliber, model M1911 pistol; the sergeants were also issued M1 rifles while the other members of the group were issued automatic pistols only. The team was told at the briefing that it would be impossible to use the airport at Hamburg and that they would have to drive two jeeps and to accompany a large truck that would be used to move the centrifuge. The trip to Hamburg was about 140 miles on what appeared on the maps to be very good roads. Brownfield, code name "Stony Black," was quick to mention that the maps are probably useless due to the constant bombing by the Allies in the Hamburg area. The maps should be helpful if the roads were recognizable and road signs were still where they belonged. It had happened in the past that retreating German soldiers would booby-trap roads and change signs and mile markers to confuse the advancing Allied forces. Brownfield ended the briefing by telling everyone to stay alert for snipers, mine fields, and trees that seem to fall accidentally just in front of their vehicle, not to mention live fighting that might erupt at any time. Brownfield then appointed Nate leader of the group until further notice and had a short-wave radio issued for communication. He finished his conversation with Nate by explaining, "Be careful, you may encounter a similar mission to yours from Russia." "They are prepared to take the needed supplies, laboratories, and scientists that our Alsos teams will be searching." "Especially it will be dangerous in your assignment in that the Russians will be crossing into the British and American zones of occupation and will probably be posing as civilians and out of their countries' uniforms."

Chapter 5

Mission, Italy

He was born Vittorio Dino Tanaka in Los Angeles, California, at the public hospital in "Japantown"—or "Japtown" as many of the locals called it. Dino was the name most of his friends used through his schooling. He did not like being called Vittorio and, more likely, the short version "VD." He recalled asking his mother if he was a "Nisei" as some of the kids had referred to him in junior high. He recalled asking his mother, "Am I a 'Nisei,' and is it a bad word?" Her response was, "Yes, you are a 'Nisei,' and no, it is not a bad word. You should be proud of it." "Your father was a 'Nisei.' I am part-Italian and part-Japanese so that makes me a 'Nisei' as well."

Dino recalled when his father was killed by a street gang of "pachucos" (Mexican thugs) during a riot when he was ten years old in Los Angeles. He and his mother were comforted by the "Japantown" community that also helped his mother maintain her flower shop. His mother was able to save enough to help pay much of his UCLA education with the help of the community and scholarships. He graduated with honors in 1937 with degrees in languages and communications and was quickly hired by the *Los Angeles Times*. He advanced quickly and soon had his own column— "Japan Town Times." The *Times* editor asked him to cover a meeting in Berlin for the signing of the "Tripartite Pact" between Japan, Germany, and Italy in 1940. The meeting turned out to be the "World War II Axis Group," which basically set the stage for the "Axis Group" declaring war against the rest of the world. The representatives at the meeting were Adolf Hitler, Benito Mussolini, and Saburo Kurusu representing each of the countries of the "Axis Group." A representative from Russia also attended the meeting but did not sign the agreement and later became part of the "Allied Group" of the United States and Great Britain.

Dino, although not part of the Japanese delegation, fit in easily with his knowledge of their languages and moved freely with the group and made several acquaintances and friends. Dino was able to utilize his language skills from UCLA—Italian, Japanese, German, French, and Spanish—which allowed him to talk to almost all of the delegations and representatives from each of the countries. At one point, the representative of the Emperor of Japan, Saburo Kurusu, asked Dino to help with some interpretations. Mr. Kurusu asked, "Dino, can you help with some translations between Japanese and Italian?" It appeared that Mr. Kurusu and Mr. Mussolini were having difficulties understanding each other. Dino was more than willing to help and became even closer to the two leaders as a result. During one of the photographic opportunities at the conference, Dino was shown standing behind the delegation of the signees of the "Tripartite," much to his and his mother's delight. It also helped sell papers back home. The picture of Dino standing behind the signatories and his article concerning the results of the conference were a real boost to Dino's reputation. Dino returned to Los Angeles to report on his findings at the conference to find that he had been promoted and his articles were being read not only locally but statewide. He had gained notice and enjoyed reporting on the affairs of Japantown. A few months later, Japan made a surprise attack on Pearl Harbor on December 7, 1941, and made it impossible for the public to believe or trust a Japanese writer. In March of 1942, he and his mother and sister were taken to a hastily built internment camp in Manzanar, California, with just three days' notice. His mother's flower shop and most of their personal belongings were confiscated with no assurance that they would ever be able to retrieve them. At the Manzanar camp, they were soon joined by thousands of other Japanese, most of whom were native-born Americans but with Japanese heritage. Dino's family was held in a small 20 × 25 enclosure with thin tarpaper walls. The camp was very primitive, high-wire fences with guard towers with armed soldiers to watch over the detainees. Death Valley was close and very appropriate for the thousands of prisoners. Their meals consisted mainly of rice and beans or some other nondescript vegetables served in a large "mess hall" with all the other prisoners at the same time as in a commune. The prisoners were eventually allowed to raise a few chickens to improve their diets. Still, not the most luxurious place to spend your confinement, especially unable to determine when or if you were to be released.

The *Los Angeles Times* printed an article about the arrest of Dino Tanaka, one of their journalists who had been accused of being a traitor to his country and imprisoned at Manzanar camp. Many readers remembered Dino as a good journalist and missed him. One in particular noted his imprisonment and contacted the camp to visit Dino. John Anello was a classmate of Dino's from UCLA and remained a friend but had little contact until it was learned that Dino had been imprisoned. The camp director allowed John to speak to Dino, but only through the fence at the entrance to the camp. John had been employed by the FBI since his graduation from UCLA and was stationed in the Los Angeles area. Several years had passed since the two men talked, but their conversation that day would lead to a new job for Dino and the movement of his family out of the camp into much better quarters provided by the Army. John described the new job as a "mission" for the cause of the country and appealed to Dino's patriotism and loyalty to the country. Dino was not being choosy; he decided within twelve seconds and said, "Yes, get me and my family out of this place."

John and Dino were required to attend extensive physical training and had to brush up on their Italian. Both men were to concentrate on the geography and history of Italy. Even more training followed at the FBI training facility in Quantico, Virginia. The two men felt better about the "mission" they were preparing for but still had no idea what they were supposed to do and where or when they were to be deployed. It mainly would be determined by the advance of Allied forces in Italy and the retreat of German forces.

In the meantime, Dino had made a quick trip back to Los Angeles to visit his mother and the newspaper where his career had begun. His time there was limited and his job at the paper was to report on issues relating to the war in Italy but he was ordered to use another journalist's name. He wrote about the reactions of the Italian citizen on the streets and their resentment to the brutality of the new regime backed by the Italian party and the "new Mussolini" that had become a "puppet" regime of the Third Reich. The citizens were even more displeased with Mussolini when in April 1942, Hitler demanded additional Italian troops to be sent to defend Germany against Russia on the Eastern Front. Mussolini sent nine divisions to the Russian front to their certain death. Casualties amounted to 85 percent either killed or captured by the Russians. The rest of the Italian Army joined the citizens of Italy in rebellion against Mussolini and on June 25, 1943, rejected Mussolini as their leader in an election. Subsequently, the King had Mussolini arrested and imprisoned. The Third Reich was not happy with the King's decision and sent a Special Forces team into the prison and helped Mussolini escape to the north of Italy to form another "puppet regime." Mussolini reigned as puppet dictator until Italian partisans captured him and most of his regime, killed them, then took their bodies to Milan to be hung by their feet on public display. Even in death Mussolini was detested by the citizens of Italy by "stoning his body" while hanging by his feet.

The "call" finally came. John and Dino were told to report to Corpus Christi Naval Air Station on August 10, 1944, for a briefing before their departure for London the following day. Both men were in Los Angeles on the 9th and decided to fly together on a commercial flight that would take them from Los Angeles to Dallas then south to Corpus Christi following a change of planes. Their mission would require that they remain in civilian clothing and work with the Italian underground. They were told that two uniformed military personnel would meet them at their gate upon arrival and take them directly to the Corpus Christi Naval Air Station. Major Powers was not taking any chances that the two men would experience the problem that Nate and Blake encountered when they arrived in Corpus Christi. No more lost soldiers or civilians to a spy network.

The trip from Corpus to RAF Mindenhall to the London safe house was uneventful but tiring and the two men arrived behind schedule the day before the briefing with Major Powers. John and Dino were surprised at the number of people in attendance. There were attendees from many areas of the country and several scientific disciplines. It made John and Dino a little nervous knowing that they would be working with highly trained professionals in physics and chemistry. Major Powers addressed the whole group first. "Welcome to London and Operation Alsos." "You and the rest of our teams will be identified tomorrow in the briefing." "In the meantime, relax but don't question or discuss your role in the mission with anyone until after the briefing at 0700." "Most of you will be leaving following the briefing for your assignments, so don't get real comfortable." The next speaker was Sergeant Smith, who was responsible for providing clothing and provisions for the first few days of the assignments. Sergeant Smith explained, "Most of you will be issued Army fatigues while some of you will be issued nondescript clothing for work with the Italian underground." "I will arrange for your transport to your assignments, provisions for the first three days, and some form of communication with this office." "It will be necessary for each team to report to Operation Alsos headquarters occasionally for further instructions or information."

The Italian Alsos Briefing

At 0700 sharp Major Powers came into the briefing room. "I trust each of you had a good night's rest. You will need it." "After today you will be in the field with your teams and assigned missions." "Communications will be handled by an assigned member of the teams and used only under extreme conditions to prevent the Germans from locating your radios through triangulation and destroying them." "That means don't talk much and use code names for your locations and team members using the radios to contact Alsos headquarters here in London." "Oh yeah, after you have used the radios, move to another location, again to prevent the enemy from locating your radios." "That is all. Good luck and Godspeed."

Sergeant Smith then made the teams' personnel assignments and described the missions to each of the teams. John and Dino were assigned the mission in Italy. Their task was to locate and confiscate a shipment of uranium ore coming from the Belgium Congo to arrive in Genoa, Italy, in five days.

John and Dino were to lead a team of two physicists from the University of Chicago who were responsible for either recruiting four Italian scientists to immigrate to the United States or making sure that they did not fall into the hands of the Russians. The two physicists would be deposited on the beach south of Genoa, Italy, by a submarine in approximately six days. John was to pose as a photographer and assistant to Dino who would pose as a journalist for an Italian newspaper. The photograph showing Dino in the background at the signing of the "Tripartite" should be a good introduction anywhere in Italy. Their forged documents, some cash, and maps would be all the team would have besides their radio during their operation. Sergeant Smith then added, "Your team will be in civilian clothes since much of Italy is still occupied by the Germans, making your mission more difficult and dangerous." "I hope you brushed up on your Italian. You are going to need it." "John and Dino, you will be dropped off the coast of Genoa by a British submarine five nights from now." "The two physicists of the team will also be dropped off the coast but further south of Genoa to be determined the next night." "You will be contacted by the Italian resistance soon after your arrival." "His code name is Enzo and he should be able to help find the shipment of ore and help determine the ship's ultimate destination." John then asked, "Will we be issued weapons?" Sergeant Smith responded, "No. If you are stopped with weapons in your possession by either the

Germans or the Italians, you could be recognized as spies and either shot or worse." John had to ask, "What's worse than being shot?" Sergeant Smith just smiled and added, "The directions just given you may change from time to time, and it's all subject to the German retreat."

John and Dino boarded a British submarine at Southampton that evening. After being directed to their quarters abort the submarine, Dino finally asked, "What have we gotten ourselves into?" John replied, "I'm not sure, but it sure beats staying in that prison camp in the California desert." Neither man had ever been underwater and dreaded the thought of being underwater for five days. Meals by themselves, no conversation with any of the crew, everything compact behind sealed steel doors did not make for a fun trip. Besides, John was claustrophobic: he didn't like tight places either. During the first night at sea, John was heard crying out in his sleep, "Help! Help! Get me out of here, I can't breathe!" Dino was able to calm John finally with several jiggers of his favorite elixir and medical stimulant, Crown Royal. The trip was purposely kept very quiet to prevent detection from the many German submarines patrolling the coast lines of Spain, North Africa, and Sicily. The five days underwater were frightening but did serve the purpose of preparing John and Dino for more dangerous enemy contact. The final day was spent preparing their cameras, maps, clothing, money, and papers they would need to work as Italian journalists and occasional underground partisans.

They finally arrived off the coast of Genoa about 0100 hours and were quickly dispatched by the crew of the submarine in a small rubber raft. The submarine submerged and left the coast, leaving John and Dino alone in the water off the coast of Genoa. Thankfully, there was no moon but the two men had no trouble maneuvering the small craft toward the coast lights of several outdoor cafés and a small hotel directly on the beach. The seas were calm with little breeze but deathly silent. Suddenly there was the sound of sirens of vehicles responding to some emergency. They first thought was that they had been discovered and the emergency lights were the authorities approaching the beach for their capture. The lights and sirens soon faded as the emergency was apparently away from the beach. The emergency vehicles moving away from the beach allowed the two men to climb the steep coastline undetected. Later, they were told that the underground had arranged the emergency so that the Alsos team could land without difficulties. Their small raft had been deflated and sank into the water, leaving no trace of the two invaders.

John motioned to Dino to follow his direction. "We were told to check into that small hotel about five hundred feet up the coast from our landing." "I would like to get something to eat, but let's check in to the hotel first." Dino had no choice but to agree and the two men were able to check in to the hotel before 0300 hours. The attendant at the desk of the hotel was surprised to see two men coming into the hotel at such a late hour, but the two men had decided to appear as two locals that had drank too much and needed some place to sober before going home. Dino and John had splashed some of their favorite elixir on their heavy cotton shirts and had not shaven for five days. The attendant became more repulsed rather than alarmed and happily provided their rooms quickly to get them out of the lobby. There was a German soldier in the lobby, seated with his chair leaning against the wall and had fallen asleep. He was supposed to be watching all the hotel guests for suspected underground activity or anyone who might look suspicious. Using his best Italian, John asked the attendant for directions to a café still open. The attendant responded, "Nothing opened this time of day. Our restaurant will open at six in the morning." As the two Alsos team members approached their room, Dino had to ask, "What am I going to do until six in the morning?" "I'm starving and all we have to eat are some K-rations." John responded, "I guess you were spoiled by the Navy food aboard the submarine." "Forget about it!" "I'll wake you up at 0600 for some breakfast. Now get some sleep."

John did not sleep. He was hungry, grumpy, and planning the next day's schedule. Dino, on the other hand, had slept like a baby even though his stomach was empty. John had awakened Dino at 0600 for some breakfast at the hotel café. The two men were to meet with their underground contact following breakfast. The two transformed Italian journalists took seats in the outside café and out of sight by prying eyes. At exactly eight, Enzo magically appeared, just like Major Powers said he would. John and Dino told Enzo about their experience the previous evening when they thought they had been exposed and the emergency vehicles were coming to capture them. Enzo finally said, "Just say thanks. We arranged a little diversion so that you could come ashore without difficulty." John and Dino did sheepishly say thanks and continued to explain their situation and the needed shipping information. Enzo responded, "You need the manifest of the Belgium Congo ship that just arrived from Pointe-Noire, Congo." "I will do my best to have the information by later this afternoon and I can meet you at a better location away from Italian and German patrols." "Here is the address. Buy an old car and be there by three o'clock." Enzo was gone just as fast as he had first appeared.

John and Dino started looking for an old car just after 0900. Taxis were rare in Genoa and most residents were riding bicycles. The two men decided to walk and to ask some of the locals for directions to a used-car dealer. Most locals again were riding bicycles out of necessity because cars used gas and rubber tires, both of which were very scarce. One old gentleman sitting outside a burned-out house was asked about a used car and he responded, "You can have mine. I have no more gas, no money, and the Germans have taken everything else." Dino responded, "We are very sorry about your house." "Do you need a place to stay or some food?" "What is your name and how can we help you?" "Can we borrow your car for a week? We will return it with a full tank of gas." The old man responded, "I will be staying with my son and he will be helping me rebuild my house." "There is a little gas in the car, but if you need more, my son can get it for you." Dino responded, "Yes, we will need more gas and your son can contact us at the Benito Hotel." "Can we leave 500 lira for your trouble?" "I know gas is expensive now. How much gas will that buy?" "We will return your car in about a week and we want to use your car for another 1,000 lira." The old man was speechless; he hadn't seen that much money in years. He then reached into his pocket and gave the keys to an old Renault parked behind his burned house. Dino then asked the old man the name of his son and to have him contact them at the Benito Hotel close to the docks before midnight. Dino then asked for directions to the address Enzo had given them for their afternoon meeting with Enzo. John and Dino now had an old car, a little gas, and directions to Enzo's house. Things were working out just like Major Powers told them they would.

Enzo's house was a short drive from the Benito Hotel. Dino parked the old Renault in front of the house next door and across the street and walked around the block checking to make sure they were not being followed before they knocked on the door to Enzo's house. Another man answered the three knocks on the door. "Come in quickly. Were you followed?" John responded, "I don't think so. There were a few pedestrians and bicycles but no military traffic."

Enzo appeared and asked if they had found a car. "It is an old Renault parked in front of the house across the street." Enzo responded, "Perfect. Where did you find that piece of junk?" John told him about the old man they had met and how they were able to find more gas. "We plan to return the car when we have completed our mission and give the old man more money to help with the rebuilding of his home." "We feel badly for the old man and hope to help him more as the Germans evacuate the area." Enzo was quick to point out, "That's very kind of you, but there are thousands like the old man you describe and we hope the Allies will push the Germans out of Italy very soon." "We will help as much as we can."

Enzo guided his guests to the back of his house before offering refreshments. Both men declined and were anxious to find the shipload of uranium. Enzo then suggested, "You need to relax a little. Take some ouzo and meet more of the other partisans in our group." John and Dino knew they had been outvoted and sat down with the three partisans beside Enzo. After some light conversation and three of four ouzo, everyone had relaxed. Enzo began the conversation about the uranium. "I was able to get a copy of the ship's manifest from the secretary of the harbor master. She is one of my cousins." "Here is something else you will need." Enzo then handed each man a German Luger pistol, ammunition, and holsters for the two pistols. Enzo then explained, "Don't ask where the Luger pistols came from. You don't want to know, and hopefully you won't need them." John and Dino thanked Enzo and began to examine the ship's manifest and were able to confirm that the ship was from Pointe-Noire, Congo, and that the cargo was the uranium ore they were seeking. The ship was the "Brazzanville" and had made port about the same time that John and Dino arrived. The manifest also indicated the shipment of 1,400 tons of uranium ore came from the mine at "Skinkolobwe" in the Belgium Congo and destined for the port at Genoa. Everything was working just like Powers said it would.

John and Dino were concerned that they were now armed with the partisan's weapons. Should they be caught by either the Italians or the Germans they would probably be shot as spies, but they took the weapons as they were told. Other news had been reported that the Allies had bombed Naples for the first mainland invasion and that the Allies had also invaded Sicily.

That meant that either more German troops would be coming south as a counterattack or running north ahead of the Allied invasion in retreat. In either case, there would be more German traffic to avoid. The Italian people were anxious to have the Germans leave their country, but Mussolini remained a staunch supporter of the Third Reich and the German Army stayed in Italy at his urging. It didn't take long for support of Mussolini and the Third Reich by the people and the Italian government to decline due to the harsh treatment of Italian citizens, the slaughter of many Italian soldiers, and the confiscation of hundreds of pieces of ancient and world-famous art and sculpture. The people of Italy were ready to shed themselves of the Third Reich.

Before John and Dino left Enzo's house, Enzo had another of the partisans fill the gas tank for their trip down the coast to find the two physicists to be dropped off the coast by another British submarine. Enzo then asked, "How many men will you pick up?" When John explained that there would be two, Enzo interrupted to add, "You will need another vehicle, and four grown men in an old Renault is crazy." Enzo then threw a key ring to Dino for another vehicle, a trusted old Fiat. As the two journalists were leaving the house, they thanked Enzo and said that they would need his help again at the many checkpoints on their way to Vienna to attend the international conference for experimental physicists. Enzo gave them a number to call when they needed his help.

The trip to Rapallo south of Genoa was about twelve miles but the old Renault could only be driven about twenty-five miles per hour before the front end began to shake, like the tires had not been balanced or had bald spots or the struts were shot or all three had not been serviced since it was purchased in 1936. Whatever the reason, the old Renault was running on its last legs. The old Fiat wasn't much better but seemed easier to drive and made the road easier to navigate. The two Alsos physicists were to be deposited on the beach much like John and Dino had been and should arrive about 2100 hours. It was still light when John and Dino reached Rapallo. They had driven the twelve miles in daylight to determine the condition of the road and to monitor German patrols and how much time it would take to arrive at Rapallo. The return trip in the dark would be a little easier. They also were concerned that the roads might have been bombed or damaged but found the roads to be in good shape. John motioned for Dino to stop at an outdoor café where they could wait the three hours until the rest of the team arrived. An outdoor café close to the beach was his choice but there were two cafés. One of the cafés was very close to the beach while the other set back about 100 meters. John did not know which restaurant would be the choice of the two arriving scientists. John agreed to sit and wait at one of the restaurants while Dino would wait at the other. There were very few patrons in either café, but it was still very early. The two men would have to wait until 1900 hours for their passengers and the traffic would be different later in the evening. Both men were well fed for the first time since arriving at Genoa while Dino had a few wines to help with his nerves.

By 1935 hours, the two physicists had not arrived and John was becoming very nervous. The larger crowd at the restaurant nearer the beach never materialized while the other café was not crowded but busy. Thanks to the war and little money to spend, both John and Dino sat comfortably and quietly waiting for the two physicists to arrive. There were a few customers sitting quietly drinking and dancing, but otherwise it was a quiet night. Finally, Eastman, one of the Chicago physicists, approached John and sat opposite him before saying anything. Finally he introduced himself and mentioned that Northcutt had joined Dino and had made their way to the cars parked behind the restaurants. "North & East" were the code names assigned to the two physicists from the University of Chicago and doctoral students of Enrico Fermi, the internationally famous Italian physicist. They were also well acquainted with the four physicists they were to help immigrate to the United States and assist in the Manhattan Project. Fortunately they all spoke fluent Italian. John was thinking that this part of the mission was going to be easy, just like Major Powers said it would.

The trip back to Genoa was slow. There was some traffic, but it was stopand-go all the way due to the high volume of German patrols guarding the shoreline. The task assigned the team was to locate the four scientists and arrange transportation from Venice, where the scientists were attending a conference of theoretical physicists in which many German and Italian scientists were gathered to discuss nuclear energy and the possibility of producing a "super weapon" for the Third Reich. The conference could be a "gold mine" to find other scientists that the Alsos Mission needed, but their mission was to find and help immigrate just the four physicists.

As the team neared the Benito Hotel, John instructed the rest of the team to park the vehicles two blocks away from the hotel and walk to the back of the hotel where John would have arranged to open the back door that was normally locked. "There is no point in exposing everyone to examination by the German guard on duty checking all hotel guests' papers." The team was able to stay close together with two team members in each room without too much discomfort. At midnight, the son of the old man whose Renault John and Dino were driving called John's room at the hotel. He had arranged for more gasoline as his father had promised. Enzo then came on the line to explain that the young man was part of the partisan group. "You can pay him tomorrow at the old grass airfield in Taggia."

The next morning, it was discovered that the shipment of

uranium ore had left the port. Dino was frantic. "How are we going to find it?" Dino returned to the hotel to tell John and the other members of the team about the missing uranium. "It's gone. The crew of the ship is standing around on the dock without a ship." John then responded, "We must contact Enzo for help." "He has a cousin on the staff of the harbor master who should be able to tell us what happened to the ship."

Uranium Shipment Disappears

It was time to call Enzo again, but before they did, they walked down to the dock to find the entire ship's crew standing around in small groups. In questioning the Belgium crew, it was learned that during the night the Belgium crew was ordered to evacuate the ship and replaced by German soldiers just before departing the port at Genoa. Dino then called for help from Enzo. Enzo had responded by contacting his cousin again with similar results. He had another manifest of the shipment and the destination was now known. Enzo and the leader of the partisan group met with Eastman and Northcutt in Dino's room to leave the manifest and to discuss any other needs of the team. Unfortunately John and Dino were still dockside and missed meeting with Enzo and Nora, the partisan leader. Nora was not happy. She explained to Enzo, "You have exposed our underground partisans in several areas, and for what, some scientists and a shipment of yellow dirt." "These Americans you are helping are costing us a fortune and what are we to receive in return?" "Do they not know a war is going on?" Enzo finally had a chance to explain after the underground leader finally ran out of breath. "The scientists are nuclear physicists trained by Enrico Fermi, the famous Italian physicist who has been helping the Americans develop a 'super bomb' before the Germans. If the Germans develop the bomb first, the whole world will be under the domination of the Third Reich." Enzo took a breath and waited to see if Nora had understood the importance of his work with the Americans. Enzo continued after a faint smile appeared on Nora's face, "The yellow dirt is uranium ore used to produce the 'super bomb' and is enough ore to make ten of the super bombs." "The Americans have agreed to supply us with any equipment and weapons we need to continue the fight against the Germans." "We are to receive our first shipment of ammunition and medical supplies tonight at the old grass airfield at Taggia." Nora responded with more of a smile at this news. She was a strikingly beautiful woman concealed in dirty dark clothing. She was tall, probably close to six feet, with long black hair that was stuffed under a black cap. She had light olive skin accentuated by hazel eyes. A strikingly beautiful woman. As she smiled the pink began to show through the soot on her face where normally makeup would be applied. Nora finally explained, "I did not know. You have done well, Enzo." "I want to meet these Americans and thank them personally." Enzo then told Nora about the next step in finding the Italian scientists. Nora responded, "You're going where?"

Chapter 6

Nate's Trip to Hamburg

Nate and his team spent the first day on the road to Hamburg moving slowly but the group made Skrydstrup-Vojens Airfield by early afternoon. They had traveled about 110 miles from the Arhus, Denmark, port and were close to the German border. The base had a small squadron of "one" Supermarine Spitfire FR.18e single-engine airplane made by VickersArmstrong, but little else. A long row of small one story buildings were their only welcoming committee, but the team finally found two mechanics that directed them to a bivouac area at the north end of the row of buildings. They had been expecting Nate's team but had made no arrangements for billet or meals or showers or anything except a place to park their vehicles out of sight of questioning eyes. The mechanics were there to keep the Spitfires running, but there were very few of them at this point and they had nothing else to repair and had left the airfield for the coast of Denmark. They informed Nate that small-arms fire had been noted several days in the past but it had been quiet since then. There had been the occasional German patrol, but little else. Most of the fighting was north where the Russians were driving the remaining German forces out of Finland. Some retreating German soldiers had been through yesterday while the aircraft was in the air and they had no idea there was anything of interest here and just passed through moving south. "You will probably run into them as you cross the border into Germany," one of the mechanics mentioned. Nate asked one of the mechanics if the group could use any of the buildings for the night. The mechanic responded, "Sure, all the doors are open and there is nothing of interest in any of them. It is shelter from the wind and rain, but that is about it."

One of the sergeants in the mission became a self-appointed dictator and began issuing orders to everyone. Prepare this, do that, and don't forget to do something else, none of which was being observed by the team members. Nate could tell that the fellow was nervous and had no idea who the people were in the team. Little did he know that there were two captains that were physicists and two civilian doctors of physics and at least one Navy SEAL in the team. None in the group really took orders well and were more accustomed to being asked politely or giving orders themselves. Nate and the other sergeant, Davis, pulled the dictator aside to have a little chat. Nate said, "I know that you don't have a clue who you are giving orders to. Maybe you should go about your own business and if someone else needs your help they will ask." "Everyone is supposed be of equal rank and we are all adults, especially the doctors and officers." The Canadian, Sergeant Cornwell, finally responded, "No one told me, I thought they were just a bunch of civilians." Nate ended the conversation by saying, "Get your head back where it belongs and leave everyone alone." The two sergeants left the meeting with Nate to prepare for their stay at the airbase. Sergeant Davis was sympathetic of the scolding that Sergeant Cornwell had received but also snickering to himself that the scene was directed at Cornwell rather than at him. The two sergeants then began preparing for their personal needs for their stay overnight. Provisions had been loaded into the truck at the airfield in Arhus for the trip to Hamburg, and each team member began rummaging as he felt the need and also found some blankets that could be useful during the night. Dr. Smitt, code name "Black," and Dr. Graff, code name "Clark," decided to explore the small village two miles from the airfield. Smitt spoke five languages while Graff spoke three but neither spoke Danish. The trip would be interesting if they could find someone who spoke one of the languages they were familiar. Nate noticed the two men leaving the bivouac area and called to them, "Where are you going? I'm supposed to watch over and protect you." The two physicists stopped and explained that they wanted to explore the village and possible find some local food. Nate continued, "You can go if you buy me a beer or three." As the three men ventured down the road toward the village, it was obvious that most people had either gone into hiding or left the town. There were very few lights and only the occasional walking person. The three men noticed an old woman sitting in a chair leaning against the wall of a small church. Graff addressed the lady in German in hopes that she would speak the language. She responded in French and said that her German was not good. Smitt knew French and asked her for directions to a tavern or pub. The old lady appeared nervous. She didn't seem to understand until Nate mimicked drinking beer from a mug. The old lady smiled and pointed with her wooden cane down the street to their right. Then she raised her cane and pointed to a faded yellow door to a small house across the street. Still speaking in French, she said, "My husband makes the best beer in town and he stocks some good wine." "Help me up. I better go with you." "Nil may shoot you before he recognizes you as American soldiers."

The little house behind the faded yellow door was rather dark and smelled of burning firewood. There were several candles arranged around the small kitchen where Nil sat reading. He was surprised to hear his wife's voice followed by heavy footsteps. He was alarmed at first but then saw that his wife was followed by three American soldiers. The old lady said,

"I told them that you made the best beer in town." Nil was a small frail man of about eighty-five but smiled constantly and did not argue with his wife. "She is right. It is the best in town." He shook each of the men's hands hardily and motioned for them to be seated. There were only four chairs and one of them had to be for the old lady. Nate graciously agreed to stand while the two physicists took the remaining two seats. In the center of the table was a large candle by which Nil had been reading, while next to it was a large pitcher of a dark brew that Nil had just poured from a wooden barrel next to the stove. The old lady was trying to reach some mugs just out of her reach when Nate volunteered to assist. The mugs were placed on the table and Nil began to pour for everyone except his wife who had explained that she was going to bed. Most of the conversation was in French and the two physicists were interpreting into English for Nate. After each interpretation, there was much laughter from the old man supposedly telling a joke that only he and the physicists understood. The beer was great and that was all that mattered to Nate. There was a small window above the kitchen sink and Nate noticed that someone was passing by on the street side of the house just below the window. Nil quickly doused the candle on the table, throwing the group into darkness. Nil told Nate to close the curtains. He then explained, "It is close to curfew and the German soldiers are clearing the streets and will be posting guards on the main road into town." Nate was first to say, "We had no idea that the area was still occupied." "Do they also check the old airfield?" Nil said that he didn't think that they did, but the guards are positioned close by. Graff explained their predicament to Nil and that they would need to return to the airfield soon but would leave early in the morning for Hamburg. After several more servings of beer and more jokes, Nil grabbed his coat and led the three out the back door. "Stay close to me and be very quiet. We will work our way around the guard in the woods." Nate checked the two physicists for their weapons which they had left at the airfield. Nice move; nothing to protect the physicists from the guard. Nate's pistol was the only weapon among the three. He also knew that gunfire would alert the other troops in the area, it was imperative that they escape without incident. As the four men crept around the guard, something alerted the guard and he was peering into the woods to identify the noise. Nate motioned for the three to proceed as planned while he lagged behind to make sure the guard did not raise an alarm. Nate stayed on the trail but hid in the dark. Nate was comfortable in the dark, part of his Navy SEAL training, while the guard was very nervous and on guard. As the guard approached the small trail leading to the airfield, he became even more nervous. He could sense the presence of something but he couldn't see anything. He pulled his flashlight from his belt and began to search the brush in front of him. It was the opportunity that Nate had been waiting. He was only a few feet from the guard who was facing the opposite direction and it was the last thing he did. Nate quickly turned the guard, took his weapon, and jabbed four fingers into the guard's throat just below the jaw. The guard could not sound an alarm and had been disarmed. Nate knew that the damage to the guard's larynx was not fatal and he did not want to kill the man. Nil came up then and delivered a six-inch butcher knife into the man's neck, severing the jugular. Nate knew that Nil made the right decision but was surprised that the eighty-five-year-old man was so physically capable. The two physicists were well ahead now but aware that Nate and Nil had disabled the guard. Nil shook their hands, pointed in the direction of the airfield, and was gone. People seem to survive war in different ways and Nil was really good at it. For his age, he was very capable of taking care of himself, guests, his home, and his wife.

As the three men approached the airfield, Nate made a command decision: move to an area where there were no German patrols. He knew that the guard would be discovered missing and other soldiers would be looking for him and could lead them in the direction of the airfield making it unsafe. He had no plan but would probably head south toward the German border and pull off the road into the trees to conceal the vehicles for the night. He decided to order Sergeant Cornwell (the NCO that had been the dictator) to check the border crossing during the night to see if their progress would be impeded or not. Nate ordered that the bivouac area be left as they had found it, gathered the team together, and moved by 2100 hours. *Wow, just like old times in the SEALs—that was close*, Nate thought to himself.

As the team left the airfield, flashlights were seen searching the brush close by the trail where the German guard had been killed, the same trail to the airfield. The guard must have been missed and the alarm had been sounded to find him and determine why he was missing. Nate had ordered silence and no lights on the vehicles as they left the airfield. It would be slow going for a while but much safer if they did not alert the German patrol. Nate was leading the team along the narrow road in the dark hoping that everyone could manage to stay on the road. Suddenly there were explosions at the airfield. The only aircraft on the field was the one remaining Spitfire F18 and the long row of low buildings parallel to the runway. Nate assumed the Germans had destroyed the airplane and possibly the buildings along the tarmac. Luckily, the mechanics where not at the airfield. The German patrol apparently thought the airfield had been temporarily used by Allied troops and had decided to destroy the airfield. The timing was perfect for Nate's team to evacuate the area and to get away before being detected and could begin moving faster using the low beam lights in front of the team. The following vehicles remained in the dark, moving cautiously but faster.

The maps provided the team indicated that the border was about fifteen miles from the airfield and they must find shelter before approaching the border crossing. Sergeant Cornwell was assigned to check the border crossing and should be returning very shortly and Nate made another decision: to stay on the road until Sergeant Cornwell returned. One of the officers, named Jackson, approached Nate, "I have visited this area before and there should be a small farm off to the north in about two miles." "The farm belonged to my wife's grandparents but should be unoccupied since they immigrated to the United States in 1938." Nate responded, "Great, let's move to the road leading to the farm and I will wait for the Sergeant Cornwell to return while you direct the rest of the team to the farmhouse." Jackson agreed and the team began to move again with the officer in the lead to help locate the road to the farm. The small road leading to the farmhouse was well hidden from the road but was located quickly. Jackson led the remaining members of the team to the old farmhouse while Nate waited for Sergeant Cornwell to return. There was no traffic on the old road, but to be safe, Nate had directed Sergeant Cornwell returning from the border crossing to use his fog lights and to watch for two flashlight flashes to signify the location of the team. Sergeant Cornwell returned in about fifteen minutes after checking the border crossing and had good news. The crossing appeared to be abandoned and no German soldiers were found on either side of the crossing. The rest of the team had been led to the farmhouse by Jackson and had found the farmhouse empty and undamaged. The farmhouse was located well off the road and should provide good shelter from any passing German patrols. As Nate and Sergeant Cornwell approached the old farmhouse, candlelight could be seen in two of the small windows and a tiny spiral trail of smoke curling upward above the chimney, a pleasant sight after driving much of the night.

First Night on the Road to Hamburg

The rest of the team had made themselves comfortable. A small fire in the fireplace, candles were found in one of the cupboards in the old kitchen, wooden boxes had been substituted for chairs around a small round table, and someone had either found or brought with them several bottles of wine. A great ending to the first day on the road to Hamburg. Jackson motioned for Nate to confer with him and the other officer. They were studying the map of Denmark and felt that they were spending the night close to the small Danish town of Hoyer, still north of the German border. It was felt that the chance of contacting any Allied troopes this far north would be slim to none. Travel in the daytime would be more dangerous than travel in the dead of night. Darkness would be their best ally. London had directed the team to contact the British Army in Holstein, about fifteen miles south of the German border and probably twenty-seven miles from their current position north of the German border. They were also directed to contact the "White Rose" resistance group in Hamburg, a student uprising group in Berlin, Hamburg, and Vienna. Radio contact was prohibited until the team was closer to Holstein and then just to confirm that Allied forces had arrived. It was concluded by the three that the trip on the following day would be at night to cover the twenty-seven miles to Holstein. Their concern now was to conceal their presence to aerial traffic during the day tomorrow.

Nate then gathered the rest of the team to discuss the need for cover of their vehicles during the day before they could leave as dark approached the next day. Everyone agreed to help conceal the vehicles and put the fire out in the fireplace in the morning, still concerned that German patrols could notice the activity at the deserted farmhouse. Nate pointed out that the trip tomorrow night would be dangerous. German patrols and possible aerial attacks by both Allied and German air forces made for dangerous roads that had been bombed continuously. Nate concluded the meeting by asking the group to make sure their weapons were in good working order and that each team member had plenty of ammunition. The first night on the road to Hamburg was to be one of the easiest of the three day trip to retrieve the centrifuge. However, it served the team well in making them very cognizant of their movements and activities of the enemy. During the three-day trip to Hamburg there were three flat tires, a dead battery, more dodging of troop movements, and finally the contact with Allied forces at Holstein. The allies were first encountered at Holstein after radio contact had been established through London. The Allied forces were a pleasant departure from the first two days on the road to Hamburg. It was good to be in the company of friendly forces and some hot food and a shower. They even found some clean clothing but no clean socks or underwear.

The Allied forces had liberated some of the area around Hamburg but the city was not totally liberated until early May 1945. There were still pockets of resistance throughout the city. Contact had been made with the resistance group, "White Rose," to help the team move around the city and especially the Hamburg campus, but their allegiance to the Americans was in question. Snipers were a constant threat and the Allied security personnel tried repeatedly to stop the team from entering the area around the university. The military police were not used to small groups of personnel brandishing papers sent from either the War Department in Washington or MI6 in London. One exhausted military policeman was busy directing traffic of military convoys, tanks, individuals in jeeps, marching military personnel, and the occasional civilian resident when Nate approached him for directions to the university. Nate explained that the small team he was leading had orders to remove a piece of equipment from the university and would appreciate any help the military policeman could spare. The policeman responded, "Are you blind? This traffic has been constant since 0600 and my replacement didn't show." "I have been told to stop all traffic to the university and I don't care if your papers are from Patton himself. You're not going to the university." Nate felt that he had met his match and decided to retreat and rethink their approach to the university. Besides, General Patton was not available to approve their move to the university. It had been confirmed that the work at the university involved isotope separation and that they had succeeded in separating uranium 235 from uranium 238 to produce the weapon-grade uranium that was so desperately needed in the Manhattan Project. The team was depressed that their mission had been stalled, but all was not lost. Smitt knew one of the professors at the university and decided to try to contact him. While Smitt was trying to contact his friend, other members of the team were attempting various means to reach the campus. Graff remembered his days on the campus and felt comfortable riding a bicycle. He asked Nate to help find a bicycle that he could approach the campus from another direction. The area around the campus was secure, but sporadic fire and the occasional shelling still disrupted all traffic. While Nate was searching for a bicycle, he heard the faint sound of a motorcycle approach from one of the recently shelled streets. The rider and his ride were dodging holes and piles of rubble and making very slow progress through the city. The rider appeared to be a British courier on a mission. Nate stopped the courier and asked for his help. After much discussion about the honorable thing to do, displaying of military orders, and threats of bodily harm, the rider agreed to help after Graff said, "Please." The courier was riding a relatively new BSA M20 motorcycle made by the Birmingham Small Arms Company—great transportation. Graff joined the motorcycle rider and away they went. Graff told the rider where to turn and how to negotiate around the troops and military barricades. Graff promised to let the courier return to his mission in twenty minutes after delivering him to the loading dock behind the physics laboratory of Hamburg University. All Nate could do now was wait. He had two of his most important physicists roaming in the rubble of Hamburg without supervision or an escort. Nate thought, *Major Powers would have a cow if he knew this was happening. What if they are captured by the Germans or Russians? Should I send someone to find them?* Nate then asked Sergeant Cornwell, the Canadian member of the team, for help. Sergeant Cornwell offered, "Give me an extra M1 rifle for Smitt and I will find him." "Does he still have his pistol?" Nate thought that he had his pistol and sent the sergeant off, chasing down Smitt, with the extra rifle. Nate had gathered the team in a bomb shelter below some sort of business a few blocks from the university campus. All members of the team were told to meet at the shelter should they be separated and all they could do now was wait for the three to return. It gave them a chance to rest and enjoy some of the K-rations they had been issued.

The first to return was Cornwell with Smitt in tow. Smitt had found a couple of local citizens who might know the professors at the university. Smitt had asked, "Do you know Professor Harteck at the University of Hamburg? He is a friend of mine." The couple admitted that they did not know Dr. Harteck personally but that most of the staff of the university had moved to a town called Hanover, about forty miles south of Hamburg. The team was tired and now disheartened. No centrifuge or Dr. Harteck—the mission was a failure. About ten minutes later, the sound of a motorcycle was heard. The courier and Graff appeared in the doorway with a box and a briefcase. Graff explained, "Some good news and some bad. The laboratory has been emptied and everyone has gone. The good news is that I was able to retrieve much of their research left behind in their hasty exit. They had been able to separate uranium 235 from uranium 238 in their small centrifuge, and they had been working on a new process of producing heavy water much faster than the older electrolysis process. The information gained from the research papers left behind by the departed physicists gave them two additional targets for needed material and scientists for subsequent Alsos missions. They had found the new process called the "Girdler sulfide process" which simplified the processing of heavy water without the required large amounts of electric power. In addition to the research papers found, there was a copy of a letter to Hitler from Himmler:

March 9, 1944, "Most Honorable Reichsmarschall . . . From this survey it may be seen that 36,000 prisoners have been put to work up to the present time in the service of the Air Force. It is planned to raise this figure to 90,000 . . . Our own quarry labor forces have been turned over for some time for utilization by the Air Force. Thus in Flossenburg former quarry labor is now working for the fighter plan program in the Messerschmitt factory at Regensburg. . . After the bombing of Regensburg the opportunity was seized to utilize the prison labor force for the immediate removal of part of the Regensburg plant . . . At the present time we are producing 900 sets of nacelles and condenser jackets per month and 120,000 parts of various kinds of the fighter plane Me 109 with a labor force of 2,000 prisoners. In Oranienburg we have assigned 6,000 prisoners to the Heinkel factory for construction of the He177. This comprises 60% of the total labor force of the factory . . .The removal of aircraft factories underground requires an additional consignment of about 100,000 prisoners. Plans for the rounding up of this labor force, in compliance with your memorandum of 2/14/44, are in full swing." (1)

This letter showed the use of prisoners of war and the use of their own people in forced labor to produce the tools of war. As early as February 1944, the German high command was robbing their own factories of personnel and equipment to be moved underground where possible. It was obvious that the Allied bombing raids were beginning to show results. Progress was being made and the need for results in the Alsos missions was becoming more important daily. Nate and his team had made some valuable contributions but needed a little rest. Nate needed to contact London for instructions. They needed to either return to Denmark or await further orders or proceed to another target or more directions from London. Too many "ors" for Nate in his current mental state. He needed a little rest.

Russian Alsos Teams in Hamburg

Alexei, team leader of team one, radioed the "Mechanic" that they had made the outskirts of Hamburg and could see the remains of St. Mary's Cathedral where they were to recover the heavy water in the basement of the cathedral. The "Mechanic" then asked, "Have you come in contact with any of the Alsos teams or T-Force teams?" Alexei responded, "No, sir. We have stayed on secondary roads and the old farm trucks are a good disguise and they do not attract attention." The "Mechanic" responded, "Be sure to stay in radio contact, but speak only in Italian, move following your transmission in case someone is listening to your message and use your code names." "Anyone listening may try to find your radio to destroy you and your radio." "Wait until nightfall before entering the city and go directly to the cathedral." "Find the heavy water and go directly to the grass airfield at Bad Oldesloe where you will be flown to Warsaw, Poland, to complete your mission." "If you encounter any American or British forces, avoid confrontation, but if you find the Alsos team, eliminate them." "Remember that your mission is very important and failure is not an option. The Western Front is not a pleasant place to spend the rest of the war should we fail."

Search for the Centrifuge

Nate found that the communications with the British headquarters on the northern outskirts of Hamburg were very cumbersome. He was finally able to contact the Alsos office in London for instructions. They were pleased with the results of the search of the laboratory but disappointed that the team did not find the centrifuge. Brownfield directed the team to continue the search for the centrifuge and to expand the search for other technical information and manufacturing facilities in the Hanover area. Brownfield's instructions included two additional physicists in the Hanover and Celle areas. Brownfield ended his conversation with Nate by asking, "Have you encountered the Russian Alsos team?" Nate was able to respond, "No, sir, we have had no contact with any Russian soldiers or teams like ours in pursuit of supplies or scientists." Nate decided the team needed a little downtime and had chosen the bomb shelter for a meeting place but would have to suffice for an overnight stay. The streets were not crowded but there were a few citizens searching for relatives or anything to help sustain life.

Cornwell and Davis were huddled in a corner of the bomb shelter away from the rest of the team when Nate approached. They were chewing on something but Nate could not tell what. Nate was about to ask for their thoughts on how to retrieve the centrifuge from the university at Hanover but changed his mind. "What are you guys eating?" Nate was having trouble concentrating on the centrifuge while some food was around. Davis answered, "My brother from Texas gave me some *hot* jerky when I left the states. Would you like some?" Nate had to decline so that the sergeants could enjoy their bounty together and uninterrupted. Without missing a beat, Nate then asked them to find something eatable for the team other than the K-ration "cardboard." "Some good German wine would be great too."

Before they could leave the team, Graff approached the three men with a suggestion. "I am very familiar with the area between here and Hanover and would like to make a suggestion on how to proceed." Nate could barely concentrate while thinking about the jerky and German wine but did finally respond. "Sure, your experience here would be really helpful." Graff began, "The allies are pushing toward Berlin and they should have already passed Bremen thirty-five miles to the southwest. If we stay on the road Bremen but turn south at Verden, we can stay clear of most military traffic. We can then approach Hanover from the northwest avoiding Bremen and Gardsen. We should be able to stay behind Allied forces all the way to Hanover." Nate then asked the two sergeants their opinion and they agreed wholeheartedly. Nate added, "We appreciate your guidance and will be asking for your direction as we leave Hamburg." Graff was pleased and walked away leaving the three men to the plans for finding some wine and food that would be more palatable than the K-rations they had been living on for three days.

Nate was tired as most of the other members of the team were. Nothing but K-rations, treated water, dirty clothes, and now more instructions and missions. Their Hamburg lodgings were not the most pleasant place to be and the Allies weren't helping. The Allied bombing caused a "firestorm" which consumed thousands of people with superheated temperatures and winds. Another thousand of inhabitants had evacuated, leaving the city almost vacant. Still sporadic gunfire, distant cannon fire, tanks belching out their noxious smoke, and still some burning buildings. He had sent the two sergeants on a mission to find some food and wine and was thinking about asking the two officers to find some blankets, clean socks, and underwear. It appeared that their current lodgings would have to suffice for a while. It might be too much to ask of the officers, but they were probably just as uncomfortable as the rest of the team. Nate decided to ask one of the officers for assistance, "Jackson, how would you feel about trying to find the team some supplies for the short stay here?" Jackson responded, "Sure, what do you think we will need." Nate then added, "Blankets, all kinds of clothing, clean socks, and underwear and anything else you can imagine to make our stay a little more comfortable." "Davis and Cornwell are searching for some food and wine." Nate then added, "We might as well make ourselves comfortable while we rest and prepare for our trip to Hanover."

Captains Jackson and Southfield left the bunker in search of the items needed by the team. Most of the items could be found at British headquarters in Hamburg, but clean socks and underwear were not to be found. On their way back to the bunker, the officers approached an old woman searching through boxes and bags in a partially burned-out store to ask for her assistance in finding underwear and socks. She answered in German that she had some underwear, but socks were impossible to find. She agreed to trade the underwear for K-rations, buttons, shoelaces, and sardines, all of which were impossible to find in Hamburg. Jackson agreed to make the trade without consulting Southfield and returned to British headquarters for the supplies she wanted. As the two captains were returning to meet with the old lady, the thought occurred to Jackson that the underwear might not be underwear the team was accustomed. The old lady met Jackson at the appointed time and place and exchanged several bags. Jackson was almost afraid to check the contents, and rightfully so: most of the underwear was ladies' pink and blue, even some with lace. Some of the laced underwear had long legs, not exactly the design the team would appreciate. There were some white too, but still ladies' underwear. Jackson and Southfield claimed them for their wardrobes without consulting the team and especially without asking Nate. They knew Nate and the other team members would not appreciate their bartered find of pink and blue underwear but reasoned that it would be better than the ten-day-old underwear they were wearing. Without the means to wash what they were wearing, the decision to wear pink or blue underwear seemed simple and automatic. They would have to make do.

Chapter 7

Italian Underground to Venice

Dion, Enzo, Northcutt, and Eastman left for Venice the next morning. Their mission was to travel the 210 miles to Venice, locate the four scientists, convince them to immigrate to the United States, and then to get them out of Venice before the Germans decided they were more valuable to Germany than to the Allies. Timing was critical; Italian resistance to the Third Reich was growing and the Allies were driving northward. The Germans were in retreat mode in some areas, but in Venice their presence at the physicists conference was intimidating. SS troops were seen at rail stations and guards were posted at many intersections of the city to control traffic into and out of the conference. The timing was more critical for the four Italian scientists. Italian partisans were hunting for Italian sympathizers working with the Germans and some had been killed while many others were publicly discredited.

The retreating Germans would not want to leave valuable sympathizers behind and if they could not take them with the retreating armies, they were to be destroyed along with their laboratories. The task of convincing the four Italian scientists to immigrate should therefore be easy, but getting them out of the country would be a real challenge.

John was to stay behind in Genoa to coordinate the shipments of medical supplies and ammunition to the underground. Many of the Belgium shipmates left behind when the Germans took their ship were frightened and worried about how to get back to their home port. John felt that they could be used if necessary to help the team and the underground move from Genoa to locate their ship. Enzo's cousin had been contacted by another underground member to get a copy of the ship's manifest, but no information was available when John met with Nora, the leader of the underground at the seaside café at the Benito Hotel. John was shocked at the introduction of Nora. "My name is John, one of the four members of a team in Italy to save four Italian scientists—" Nora interrupted, "I know who you are and what you are doing." "I wanted to meet you myself, to thank you, and to help with the receipt of the much-needed supplies and ammunition tonight." John finally responded, "You are not what I expected." Nora had changed from her dark drab camouflaged clothing to a bright yellow dress with a blue waistband and blue ribbon to keep her long black hair away from her face. She was strikingly beautiful and tall. Wearing high heels made her look even more impressive. Not what you would expect for an underground leader. Nora and John were discussing the trip to the grass airfield when Enzo arrived. "Everything has been prepared." "Be at my house this evening at 9:30 for the trip to the airfield." As Enzo and Nora left the hotel, John was still admiring the beautiful leader of the underground and anticipating their meeting that evening. He had the feeling that this would be a good meeting.

Enzo had John transported by another member of the underground to the house where John had met with Enzo after their first meeting. Nora welcomed John at the door and motioned for him to follow her to the back of the house where several old vehicles were assembled. She was not wearing her yellow dress and high heels. The camouflaged dark apparel appeared like a tall skinny kid hiding under a tent that had collapsed. Not like their first meeting. Nora and John were placed in the backseat of an old brown fiat while a driver and an armed guard sat in the front seat. There were two other smaller cars and a large farm vehicle driven by Enzo in the convoy that John could not identify. Probably another Fiat. Should be enough space for the shipment to arrive in four hours at the old grass airfield. The trip to the airfield was long and really pleasant with Nora and John talking and comparing war stories. John had become infatuated by this woman. The group arrived at the old airfield before the appointed time to prepare a "drop zone" for the aircraft to deliver the supplies. The plane was not going to land, but will drop the supplies by parachute from about two hundred feet. The "drop zone" was to be a cross outlined in white lights with one large red light in the intersection of the cross bars. London had specified the red light because of an incident the previous week where the Germans had intercepted the instructions for a similar cross without a red marker on a nonsecured radio call. The instructions this time were on a secure line and specified the red marker. The earlier mistake cost a vital shipment to another underground group and several of its members were captured. London said it wasn't supposed to happen like that.

The trip to the grass airfield at Taggia was slowed by moving with low beam lights, but still made the seventy-mile trip in about two hours. The road parallels the coast line through many small villages but no German patrol or checkpoints were encountered.

The battery-powered lights were illuminated just five minutes before the appointed time for the plane to arrive. It took the team several minutes to place the lights in the shape of a cross and the red marker in the center. The team then turned on the lights within the specified time as a precaution that London had demanded to prevent German intervention if they should observe the lights. The instructions also asked that the lights be extinguished immediately after the drop for the same reason. John was watching the western horizon when he heard the rumble of the plane's engines. "There it is, coming from the northwest." The plane was traveling at a very low altitude and a very slow speed to drop the supplies as closely as possible to the "drop zone." The drop was made after one pass and Nora ordered the lights to be extinguished. The drop was completed and the plane disappeared, heading southeast. The hunt was on now for the parachutes and pods with the equipment and supplies. It took about thirty minutes to locate all the pods of supplies and load them into the old farm truck. The parachutes were buried and covered with dead leaves and branches. John observed, "Looks like nothing happened here tonight. Good work." "Let's get out of here before someone alerts a German patrol." Enzo had prepared a vehicle for John's trip to Marseille in pursuit of the shipment of uranium ore. From there the destination was unknown. John approached both Enzo and Nora for their final departure. "Thanks for your help and I look forward to seeing you again." Nora placed a light kiss on John's left cheek while Enzo squeezed his hand. "Until we meet again." With their good-byes, Nora and Enzo disappeared into the night.

John's trip to Marseille went smoothly following the instructions and maps that Enzo had provided. He couldn't get Nora out of his mind. What a beautiful woman. There were so many questions John had wanted to discuss with Nora, almost none relating to their underground activities.

He finally resigned to the fact that he probably would not see her again. Maybe after the war. When he reached Marseille, he radioed London for instructions. He most likely would be called back to Venice to assist Dino, but he was a long way from Venice. Major Powers came on the radio. "Nice work, John. Now get your butt back here to London. We need you here to get ready for the next mission." "You and Dino will be returning to Marseille in a few days in search of the 1,400 tons of uranium ore." John then asked, "How?" Major Powers then pointed out, "You remember that airfield at Taggia? A transport will pick you up at 0100 tomorrow morning." "Be there on time."

The Venice Physicists Conference

It was a different story in Venice. SS troops everywhere, Italian soldiers and police directing traffic, and official chauffeured automobiles going to and coming from the conference center.

Enzo had a plan that might work. They decided to park their vehicles seven miles out of town on the Padova highway. From there, Enzo's associates would transport the team to a warehouse owned by a vegetable company where a truck would be made available for them. Enzo had a cousin on the police force and he might be persuaded to help rent or steal one of the chauffeured automobiles to deliver Northcutt and Eastman to the conference. Dino found a black suit belonging to one of the waiters at a local café that probably wouldn't be needed until dinner and he figured they might as well get some use from it. Enzo's cousin was able to "borrow" one of the black automobiles that looked official and gave the keys to Enzo for 500 lira. Dino then thought, *It's amazing what a little bribe can buy.* Enzo tried the suit for fit, but he could not button the shirt and the belt was too short. That left Dino to become the driver of the chauffeured limousine. It wasn't because Dino was uncomfortable talking with the officials at the entrance of the conference, it was because Enzo was uncomfortable in the clothes of the driver of the limousine. Enzo was left behind to make the preparations for the vegetable truck to transport the physicists away from the conference. Enzo then thought, *This is one time when my waistline came in handy in getting me out of some unpleasant work.*

The conference was to open officially at 0900 and many of the attendees had arrived earlier for breakfast before the opening. Dino had been watching the police officers and the SS as they monitored the traffic into the conference. His plan was to wait until the conference opened and a much larger amount of traffic would help conceal the driver and passengers. He noticed that the police officers were asking for the papers of the driver only and not the passengers. Should make the trip to deposit the two scientists at the front door easy, although if they were questioned, they were to represent themselves as Italian physicists. He felt assured that he would not be questioned by the authorities at the conference due to the large volume of traffic. The SS officers were a different matter. They stood in small groups in their usual black leather looking superior and basically doing nothing but appearing bored. Maybe they were concerned that the Allies were gaining ground and that their stay in Italy may be terminated at any time. Dino finally told the scientists, "Be careful, there are SS soldiers everywhere." "Enzo will be driving a red Vermicelli vegetable delivery truck at the loading dock at the back of the building at 1300 hours. Each of you take two of the Italian physicists at a time to the back of the building and take a seat in the covered back of the truck." "Wait five minutes between each group leaving the conference floor." "Enzo will then load empty crates in front of you." "The SS or the Italian police are not inspecting departing vehicles, but they may and you need to be concealed behind the boxes." "Enzo has concealed a German Luger in the back sidewall of the truck should you need it." "Good luck and we will meet you at the warehouse by 1400 hours."

The conference was well attended especially with a war in progress. However, most of the attendees were not Italian. They came from all countries that the Germans had annexed, even some Japanese attendees, but mainly German. The four scientists were tending the booth of the Ca Foscari University and experiencing very little traffic. Northcutt and Eastman approached the booth and began discussing physics in general before retreating to their real purpose for being at the conference. Northcutt was able to discuss their plans fairly openly while Eastman kept watch for other attendees and officials of the conference. Three of the Italian physicists were easily convinced to join the team to leave the conference while the fourth agreed to go but was reluctant and kept watching the crowd supposedly for police or officials. The time was fast approaching when the first pair of Italian scientists were to leave the booth and proceed to the back of the conference building. At 1230 hours, the first of the two physicists were to leave for the back of the conference floor for the loading dock. Enzo had parked his truck and unloaded the vegetables with the help of two underground associates. Northcutt was the leader of the first pair of scientists to approach the dock and was directed by Enzo into the back of the truck. Eastman was next and he brought the reluctant physicist with him. Time seemed to stand still for Enzo. Another five minutes passed and still waiting for the last pair of scientist to arrive at the dock. The wait was excruciatingly painful, but the time came and the last pair left the conference floor for the back of the building. Enzo was frantic when the final pair finally took their seats in the back of the vegetable truck. Several SS officers had walked by the loading dock but had not stopped anyone for questioning and continued to appear bored. Enzo began loading the empty crates into the truck when the reluctant Italian scientist began to complain and attempted to get out of the truck. Enzo and his associates grabbed the young scientist and wrestled him to the floor of the truck where Northcutt took over. The weapon that Enzo had placed in the side panel was used as a club to silence the reluctant scientist. The now-unconscious young man could be dealt with later after they left the conference.

All of the Alsos team, Enzo and his two associates gathered at the vegetable warehouse where they took a well-deserved break before the trip back to their vehicles on the Padova highway. Dino had been busy trying to arrange the transport of the four scientists out of the country. He had used their short-wave radio to contact London for instructions. He then moved to another location and waited for a response to avoid the German attempts to locate radios by triangulation and to destroy them. The new instructions came about twenty minutes later. They were to proceed to Ferrara about seventy miles southwest of Venice to a grass airfield 1.8 miles north of the village of Bondene, which is just north of Ferrara. At 2030 hours they would arrange a lighted field for an Avro Lancaster X transport to pick up all team members and Italian scientists to be flown to Palermo where their mission will be completed.

Once their instructions were complete, Major Brownfield exhorted, "Good luck and God speed!"

After the new directions were discussed with the team and the partisans, it was decided that the reluctant physicist would "disappear" at the hands of the partisans and the team would use the truck to transport the team and the three scientists to Ferrara. Dino made a special request of Enzo: to thank Nora for the support of all the underground and to return the Renault to the old man in Genoa along with 1,000 lira. John was still in Marseille now after helping the underground with needed supplies and would be flown out by a similar transport from the grass airfield at Taggia.

Chapter 8

London Debriefing: Italy

Majors Powers and Brownfield were pleased with the performance of the Italian Alsos team. They had completed their assignment and had demonstrated the following results:

1. The Alsos team in Italy was able to complete its assignment of immigrating several very important physicists. It was fortunate that the single physicist who would not immigrate had not fallen into the hands of the Russians.

2. The Alsos team in Italy tracked the uranium ore shipment from the Belgium Congo to Genoa then to Arles, France, for further processing. Ultimate destination unknown, but the next mission was to locate the 1,400 tons of uranium wherever it was.

3. The Alsos team in Italy was able to contact the Italian underground and cement relations with this valuable asset. The Italian underground is now a valuable ally.

Major Powers went on to say, "The Italian team performed admirably and completed its mission successfully and in a timely manner." "You can now take a short holiday and have a good time." "Your next assignment will be divulged to you in two days." "Go have some fun but don't be late for your briefing at 0730 day after tomorrow." "Dismissed."

Dino and the team decided to headquarter at the London Safe House but to spend most of their time off in the sidewalk cafés and visit a few night spots for entertainment. They were missing John, who was still in Marseille, but he probably would meet them during the next day. The next mission was to be announced at the briefing the day after tomorrow.

Chapter 9

Nate's Team Moves to Hanover

Everyone hated to leave Hamburg and their lovely bomb shelter and pink and blue underwear (some with lace). Such is life in the line of duty. At the suggestion of Graff who had been a student at Hamburg University, the team was to travel southwest toward Bremen but stay off the main roads to avoid the masses of Allied military traffic. Graff had suggested to take the cutoff at Rotenburg and head south toward Verden before heading southeast toward Hanover, which would avoid much traffic in the Bremen area. The trip to Rotenburg was against the Allied traffic and went smoothly. When the team turned south at Rotenburg, it was a different story. The roads were narrow country roads with little to no traffic for most of the way to Verden. About four miles from Verden, a wandering small group of German soldiers was encountered. As the lead jeep topped a hill on the narrow road, a small group of German soldiers scattered into the woods. Nate was driving the lead jeep and came to a screeching halt. About two hundred yards separated the jeep from the German soldiers, which made Nate very nervous, but instead of quickly driving in reverse, everyone jumped out of the jeep and took refuge. Without warning, one of the German soldiers raised his weapon with a piece of white fabric attached to the barrel and his other arm was raised in surrender. Three other German soldiers joined the first and stood by the road waiting for instructions. Nate asked Otto to tell them to lay their weapons on the ground and place both hands on their heads. Just as quickly, Davis and Cornwell moved toward the soldiers with their weapons directed at the group. The German troops were ordered to drop their weapons and proceed in the direction of short rock wall and ordered them to take a seat on the ground. The team now had four prisoners and no place to keep them. Nate then asked Davis to find some shelter for the approaching night where the party could wait for Hamburg headquarters to send a transport for the prisoners. While Cornwell guarded the prisoners, Davis had found an old farmhouse off the road about three hundred yards that appeared abandoned. Nate addressed the rest of the team, "Looks like we are to sit with surrendered soldiers for a while." He then asked Jackson, "Contact the British headquarters in Hamburg for assistance in handling the prisoners." Jackson quickly contacted the British headquarters but had bad news. "The British are moving out of Hamburg heading southeast toward Hanover and could not help but did volunteer to call the American 6th Army in Paris to report our situation." Nate then said, "Probably be here sometime, might as well see what we can find in the old house." Cornwell and Davis guarded the prisoners while the two captains and the physicists began searching the house. Jackson had found some canned fruit and vegetables while Otto had found some wine stored in the basement and several candles. Graff reported finding a room without windows and a heavy door that would serve nicely as a jail for the prisoners until help arrived. There was no water or electricity but the house was great cover from the elements. Cornwell and Davis then marched the prisoners off the road toward the house to deposit them in the small room. Nate was thinking, *This will do nicely for the night, but it really slows our progress toward Hanover.* Otto and Graff were outside gathering wood for the fire when they were approached by another group of seven surrendering German soldiers. Neither of the doctors had their weapons but observed that the Germans were displaying a white flag of surrender. Graff ordered the soldiers to drop their weapons and place their hands over their heads while Otto ran for help. "We have more prisoners." Davis and Cornwell responded quickly and gathered the new group of prisoners and had them seated as Nate approached. "What can we do with them?" Davis then volunteered. "The room we have the other prisoners is too small. We may have to move them into the basement." Nate agreed and then asked everyone else to help empty the basement of anything they needed or could be used as a weapon. Shortly, the basement was empty. Davis escorted the four prisoners from the small room to the basement while Cornwell held the new prisoners at bay. When Davis returned, the two sergeants led the new prisoners into the house and down into the basement. Nate felt that time was being wasted and decided to call the American 6th Army Headquarters in Paris himself. He had never been accused of being overly patient. Strangely enough, Nate was told that two trucks were on their way to take the prisoners into custody. The British actually had called for help and he had the audacity of questioning their audacity (whatever that means). Upon questioning one of the German soldiers, Nate learned that their battle group had been overrun by American troops and that they were left behind not knowing where their group was located. Probably retreating toward Hanover. It was time for the group to decide whether to stay where they were or try to move closer to Hanover. The team said in unison, "Let's stay here tonight."

Where Is the Centrifuge?

Two trucks from 3rd Army Headquarters rolled into the front of the old farmhouse at 2100 hours. The trucks already had fifteen prisoners in custody found on the road from Paris. The guards were tired, grumpy, and needing a little rest and food to reenergize, and they decided to stay the night and return to Paris in the morning. It was decided by the team and the guards that the best place for the twenty-two prisoners for the overnight stay would be the basement after they had removed any items from the new prisoners that could be used as a weapon. The work went smoothly with most of the team participating. Cornwell and Davis carried weapons and began moving the prisoners down the stairs leading to the basement when a scuffle between three prisoners was heard at the bottom of the stairs. One of the prisoners was dragged down to the ground by two other prisoners before Davis could intervene. Graff was called to speak to the prisoners in German. "What has happened?" "What's going on?" The two prisoners who wrestled the third prisoner to the ground responded, "This crazy Hitler Youth was trying to escape and wanted to continue to fight." "He is fourteen years old and stupid." Graff responded, "Bring him back to the small room on the first floor." "We will keep him separate from the rest of the prisoners." Davis took the Hitler Youth into his custody and placed him in the smaller room. Graff followed Davis and the Hitler Youth into the smaller room and began questioning him. "How old are you?" "Have you eaten recently?" "Why do you still wish to continue fighting a lost war?" To which the Hitler Youth replied, "No, we have not eaten for three days while we have been hiding in the woods since our battle group was overtaken by the American Army." "I am almost fifteen years old and ready to fight to the death." Graff then offered the young man some of the food and water that had been gathered to serve the team and the prisoners. Graff added, "Wouldn't you rather stop fighting and go back home to your family and friends and forget the war?" The Hitler Youth was still very antagonistic and visibly angry at his captors and everything in general. Graff sadly closed the door and left the young man alone with his thoughts.

Jackson and Nate had prepared some small portions of the vegetables and fruit that had been found in the basement. Some K-rations had been packed for the team and the truck drivers also had a few K-ration "cardboard" which could be shared with the prisoners. Nate reasoned that the wine would be shared by the Alsos team only; after all, the drivers of the two trucks should not drink and drive. Especially since the wine was running low. Before Graff turned in for the night he wanted to speak to the Hitler Youth again. Graff went to the door of the small room, knocked and entered without waiting for a response. The young man was awake and sitting on the cold floor with a blanket wrapped around him. The prisoner seemed to have settled into his captivity and had forgotten the anger that had welled up in him so very easily just two hours earlier. Being hungry and thirsty added to his discomfort. Graff introduced himself and mentioned that he was born in Germany, attended schools in the Berlin area, and attended the University at Hamburg. He then asked the youth, "Do you intend to attend college when the war is over?" The Hitler Youth finally answered, "Possibly. My father is a professor at University of Hamburg and my grandfather also taught there." Graff felt the tension leave the young man and then asked, "Who is your father?" "I may have known him. I studied physics there and received my doctorate in theoretical physics there." The Hitler Youth then responded, "My father teaches chemistry and his name is Wilhelm Moth and he is a member of the Uranium Club." "My grandfather taught philosophy before he died in 1938." Graff was shocked. He had several classes with and had been a roommate for a short time with the younger Dr. Moth and his name was on the list of scientists needed by the Alsos Mission. The older Dr. Moth had taught philosophy and Graff took two classes under him. Graff then asked, "Do you know where your family and your father are now?" "It's been fifteen years since I attended school with your father." "Your father should know Dr. Paul Martek, a friend and also a professor of mine from Hamburg." The young man was trying to remain "tough" but it was obvious that he was tired of the war and would like to go home. "My father and Dr. Martek have moved from the University of Hamburg because of the constant bombing and have moved the laboratory to Hanover, but I think he and Dr. Martek have moved again to Celle with a small laboratory staff." Graff then asked, "If you would like, we can take you to your father, it is on the way to our destination." When Graff left the room, he thought he heard the young man sobbing, or more likely just snoring.

A small fire had been built in the fireplace before everyone settled down for the evening. It would be necessary for guards to be posted during the night; Davis and Cornwell handled the details of posting the guards. The team was still about 120 miles from Hanover and the burden of the prisoners was slowing their progress. The old farmhouse was about five miles from Verden. Verden would be passed on their way to Hanover. Nate and Jackson were planning to travel to Verden, turn southeast and parallel to the Aller River to Walsrode, then south toward Hanover in the hopes that the bridge over the Aller River was still standing. Nate reasoned, "If that bridge has been destroyed the team would have to backtrack west to Walsrode and cross the Aller River at Schwarmstedt." Nate and Jackson were still planning their trip tomorrow when Graff approached the two men, "We need to change our plans for our trip to Hanover. We need to go to the village of Celle thirty miles north of Hanover." Nate had to ask, "I hope you have a good reason for the detour. I thought we were to retrieve the centrifuge in Hanover." Graff responded, "The Hitler Youth we captured is acquainted with Drs. Moth and Martek. In fact his father is the younger of two professors at Hamburg University." "The Hitler Youth claims that Dr. Moth is his father and that the laboratory and the centrifuge have been moved from Hanover to Celle." "I'm sure they would not leave there centrifuge with anyone else." "The laboratory at Hanover is still important, but we can find the centrifuge and two of the scientists before we proceed to Hanover." Nate had to agree, "On the map, Celle and Hanover are about the same distance from our current location, we can make the trip a triangle and avoid the crossing of the Aller River at Walsrode." "Take the scientists into custody along with the centrifuge then head toward Hanover for the laboratory at the University of Hanover." Davis and Cornwell responded in unison, "Sounds like a plan."

Jackson then explained, "We will need to radio the 6th Army Headquarters in Paris for more equipment and personnel to handle the centrifuge and take the scientists into custody." Nate then added, "Yes, radio Paris for the equipment. It's too late to leave for Celle tonight anyway and we need to help control the prisoners until the truck drivers and guards are able to leave in the morning." "We should wait until we have the necessary equipment and personnel before we leave." "That will give us a little time to rest."

Suddenly, there was small-arms gunfire heard. The guard came into the house to report that someone had shot a flare into the air and had illuminated the area about five hundred yards from the old house. The gunfire was in response to the light. "We need to be prepared for company," the guard reported.

"Our jeeps are out of sight, but the two big trucks will give away our position should they continue to come down the road." Everyone scrambled to find their weapons and helmets. The two truck drivers approached Nate. "Should we move our trucks further into the woods?"

Nate directed them to move the trucks if they could do so very quietly. "On the other hand, the two large trucks would indicate a fairly large contingent of soldiers and might just keep the enemy from approaching." Davis and Cornwell disagreed. "Move the trucks. We will need them and if they can't see us or the trucks, they will probably pass without noticing." "But we need to be prepared for company." Nate then noted, "We must make sure the prisoners are quiet and do not alert whoever the company might be."

Everyone was quiet and ready for action. The team, the truck drivers, and guards were positioned at the windows and the candles had been doused. The trucks had been quietly moved into the woods and out of sight. The fire had been doused with some water and was no longer showing any smoke from the smoke stack. It was eerily quiet with bright moonlight making the dirt road appear as a gray ribbon fading off into the night. The sound of an approaching engine broke the silence. It was distant, but it was getting closer. Cornwell recognized the sound and whispered, "It's a small tank. It's not a Bradley, or a Panzer Tiger." "Sounds like a six-cylinder engine. Must be a light British or French tank." The tank was approaching from the north heading south toward the road to Hanover. As it approached everyone was quiet and very alert. The lights on the tank were illuminated and moving very slowly followed by German prisoners. A French soldier was mounted on the back of the tank guarding the German prisoners. Nate finally whispered, "Looks like a French tank and captured prisoners followed by a large truck with more French soldiers aboard." Cornwell then added, "It is a small French tank, I think a Char B1 with a six-cylinder Renault engine." Davis then asked, "Should we let them know we are here? They could take our prisoners and we could use the two trucks from 6th Army Headquarters to move the centrifuge from Celle." Nate made a quick command decision: "Yes, we can dispose of our prisoners and the two trucks from the 6th Army Headquarters can help take the captives to Paris." "That would relive the tank to resume the battle or find more prisoners." Sounded like a really good plan until Davis was ordered to halt by the French soldier on the tank and to place his hands on his head. The French soldier had ordered the tank to stop while Davis hollered "Americains" as the tank rolled to a stop. The tank commander responding to the alert by rotating his gun in the direction of Davis. The prisoners had also responded by dropping to the ground. Just as quickly, the French soldiers in the truck dismounted and were pointing their weapons at Davis. Davis was joined by Otto, both fluent in French. "Americains, Americains, soldats Americains. Don't fire on the soldats Americains." Everyone seemed to relax as the tank commander shut down his engine and walked toward Davis and Otto. The tank commander introduced himself and apologized profusely before Davis could explain their situation. Both Otto and Davis began to explain their predicament in French and then asked the commander to take the their prisoners to the internment camps in exchange for transportation for all the captives in the two large American trucks that Paris had sent, all the while hoping the tank was taking the prisoners to 6th Army Headquarters. As it turned out, the tank commander was headed toward Paris but the Allies had established another internment camp closer to the German border but still about ninety miles and too far for the prisoners to walk. Nate joined the small group and offered, "Looks like you and your men could stand to take a break." "We can post a guard to watch your prisoners while you and your men relax for a while." "We can also arrange for the two American trucks to be transferred to you to move your captives much faster and safer." The tank commander responded, "Oui, oui." "I accept your generous offer of the trucks and especially the time to take a break." "There are many more prisoners and villagers on the road from Hanover." "My orders are to move the prisoners to the internment camp and to help as many of the villagers as possible." "I am almost out of gas and would have to stop shortly anyway." Nate responded, "We don't have any diesel fuel, but if you are running of gasoline, we could leave you several jerricans." "We are headed to Celle and should be able to replenish our fuel supply there or have some diesel fuel sent to you from one of the advanced supply depots." The tank commander was very grateful but admitted that he had already made a request for more diesel fuel and should arrive by noon tomorrow. He then offered a stash of German wine he had confiscated from the German officers in his group of captives. "If you need any weapons too, we have many stored in the tank belonging to the prisoners." Nate then asked Davis to arrange to guard the prisoners while the French soldiers took a break. Nate asked Graff and Otto to find the German officers the tank commander had mentioned and question them about battle plans or information that might yield any needed supplies, uranium, or physicists. Nate then thought to himself, *That's all we need is more targets of needed supplies.* As Graff and Otto approached the prisoners, they were speaking in English. They asked the prisoners, "Who among you are the officers?" There was no response. "We were told that there were officers in your group." Still no response. The prisoners were seated on the ground and not comfortable. Finally, Otto could hear whispers in German about changing uniforms with an officer before being captured. The prisoners did not know that Graff and Otto could understand German and continued to complain about having to change uniforms with the officers to conceal their identity. Two of the prisoners were moving nervously and kept their heads down to avoid recognition. Graff finally said in German, "Are these two your officers? Your uniform is a little baggy on you."

Almost in unison, the other prisoners said yes and pointed to the other guilty party, also in an ill-fitting uniform. Otto then asked one of the armed guards to take the two officers into the old farmhouse for questioning. "Place them in the small room with the Hitler Youth until I have a chance to question them." Jackson was an experienced interrogator but did not speak German. He asked Otto to repeat his questions of the officers in German. It was obvious that the two officers were through fighting and were very cooperative, but maybe too cooperative. Much of the information they gave to Otto would have to be verified before any action taken based on the information gained in the interviews. They learned that the German forces had retreated to three miles west of Hanover and Celle and the departing German forces had blown the bridges at Schwarmstedt over the Aller River, thus cutting off the access to Hanover from the northwest. This information confirmed that their plan to avoid crossing the river north of Schwarmstedt was confirmed and that the team should go directly east toward Celle. The officers were not sure of the number of German soldiers, but there were about fifty Panzer Tiger tanks and perhaps a thousand soldiers under a general. There were several other pockets of German soldiers marooned between the old farmhouse and the German line established outside of Hanover and any Allied troops should be wary of their presence. The captives did not divulge any other information to help the team locate more Alsos objectives. The Germans were surrendering to American troops rather than facing the wrath of the German officers who had been shooting deserters. Deserters were especially avoiding the Russian troops for fear of being captured and tortured. Apparently the British, French, and American Allies were treating the captives much better than the Russians. It was no surprise, considering how poorly the Germans had treated captured Russians on the Eastern Front. Jackson had completed his interrogation of the two officers and made sure the truck drivers and guards taking the prisoners to the internment camp were aware of their identities and to have them interrogated again. Of course the Hitler Youth had been present during the interrogation of the two officers although they were questioned one at a time out of the presence of the other. The Hitler Youth had to face the reality that to continue fighting was futile.

Russian Team Leaves Hamburg

"Dig it out quickly!" Matrei, one of the Russian Alsos team leaders whispered. "The barrels of heavy water are there, under the broken glass and wooden beams." "It will be light soon. Hurry, but be quiet." The heavy water was located quickly where they were told it would be: in the basement of the bomb-damaged St. Mary's Cathedral. "Be quiet and quick. We must not alert either the British or American forces that have occupied the city." The Russian team worked quickly to remove the heavy water and were preparing to proceed to the University of Hamburg to capture Drs. Gerlach and Harteck as Alexie returned from his trip to the university to see if the two doctors were still there and could be taken. He had bad news. "The American Alsos team and a large T-Force team is loading some laboratory equipment, and it is reported by Klaus that the centrifuge and the two doctors have moved to Hanover."

The two old farm vehicles with their precious load of heavy water pulled away from the damaged cathedral and headed for the grass airfield at Bad Oldesloe. Matrei and Alexie were disappointed that the two physicists and the centrifuge were not available to be taken, but they did succeed in securing the necessary heavy water to operate the nuclear pile safely. They were approaching the small hotel Schanzenstern when an American Army guard ordered them to stop. Materei tensed and prepared to eliminate the guard with his weapon pointed at his midsection through the door of the old truck. The American guard had been ordered to check all traffic through the city and had routinely stopped the farm trucks without saying anything to the driver. He proceeded to check the back of the trucks for deserters or weapons and found only barrels of something in French that he could not read. The guard then approached the door of the truck to ask for their papers. Materei then volunteered and said, "We have no papers." "We are taking kerosene to our village to fuel our heaters." "There has been no coal since the war and we are preparing for cold to continue for another two months." The guard was surprised that the driver spoke English and just waved the two trucks to be on their way.

Near sunrise, the two farm trucks left Hamburg for Bad Oldesloe. Maerei radioed the "Mechanic" to alert him to the success of their mission. The "Mechanic" responded, "Good work, comrade, you have done well." "There is enough heavy water moderator now in our possession to produce a successful nuclear pile." "Moscow was also pleased." "The transport should be landing at the grass airfield in one hour. Get your cargo loaded and take a well-earned break, and thank your teams for me."

As the team was loading their cargo onto the transport, the radio once again began to speak. The "Mechanic" interrupted their work with more instructions. "A message has just received from our source, Klaus at the American Alsos headquarters, that there is a significant source of uranium and thorium metals located in the bombed plant in Oranienburg." "On March 15 the Allies bombed the plant, but we are told that a supply of both metals has been uncovered and needed by our physicists to produce our super bomb." The "Mechanic" then ordered the teams to proceed to Oranienburg rather than the promised break. "Materei and Vasily, take the two trucks and four men with you to retrieve the estimated twelve tons of uranium and an undisclosed amount of thorium metals." "Load the materials found and quickly leave for the Polish border town of Szczecin where the cargo will be taken by ship to the port of Riga." "You and your team will board the ship for the trip home." "You should not have any difficulty with American or British troops since this area is already in Russian control and some twelve miles north of Berlin."

"Are there any questions?" asked the "Mechanic." Vasily, one of the team leaders then asked, "What will become of the nine railcars of uranium oxide in Toulouse and the cyclotron parts and uranium oxide in Strasbourg?" The "Mechanic" was prepared for the question. "Special Forces have been assigned those two targets and not of our concern, but I would assume they will be attacked or taken by local saboteurs or French underground forces." "Special Forces have also been charged with the destruction of the Messerschmitt factory in Regensburg that is being built underground where many of the various German aircraft are being built." "The other aircraft facility at Sankt Georgen an der Gusen, Austria is also targeted by Special Forces." "Both of the aircraft facilities use slave labor from KZ Gusen 1 and 2 camps of nearby Mauthausen concentration camp." "It is estimated that forty thousand to eighty thousand concentration camp laborers will be liberated as these two plants are destroyed." "Unfortunately, those who remain in German captivity will be returned to the concentration camps and certain destruction if not liberated by the Allied forces very soon." "Those slave laborers who successfully escape German captivity have a good chance to survive if found quickly by the Allied forces." "A captured letter found in a stack of documents placed on my desk explains much of the horrors of the use of slave labor from German-occupied countries." "Also, captured Russian, Italian, and American soldiers are used and returned daily to the concentration camps." "It is a letter addressed to Himmler from Goering dated February 1944:

TOP SECRET

"I should like to request that you place at my disposal the largest possible number of concentration camp prisoners for work in aircraft production, since past experience has shown this manpower to be especially well suited for utilization. Present air attacks necessitate the removal of industry underground. Concentration camp prisoners provide an excellent source of labor supply as they are already rounded up and can be quartered in such a way as to make them readily available . . . Heil Hitler! Your Goering, Reichmarshal of the Great German Reich." (2)

Take a Break

At the same time as the interrogation of the officers was proceeding, the tank commander told his men to take a break as he headed to the tank for the confiscated wine. Nate was speaking to the team, "We can't move toward Celle yet. We have company to entertain. Might as well relax and enjoy our break too."

The prisoners were placed in the basement and smaller room on the first floor with the Hitler Youth along with the two German officers. Should make for great conversation between captured soldiers and their deceitful leaders and the Hitler Youth who wants to go home. The team and French soldiers still had some provisions which they shared with the prisoners, but the fine German wine that the French tank commander had found was not shared with the prisoners. It was late when everyone tried to get some sleep. Nate had posted a guard and Davis had arranged an hour changing of the guard so that everyone should be able to get some needed rest. The French commander arranged for his own guards to supplement guards that Davis had posted. Nate finally had time to relax. He had no plans to make today or for the next few days. He was thinking about home for a change. He wondered how Blake was faring in his assignment in Paris and whether he had tried to stay in contact with his new wife, Vivian, back home. Blake and Vivian had just been married a few months before

Blake had been called back to service in Operation Alsos. Nate was thinking about the great little business he had started with Brandon, the retired editor of the *Mountain Mail*. The little hamburger restaurant he and Brandon had started and the beautiful blue Chevy pickup the FBI had given them for their help in capturing several saboteurs in the desert in southern New Mexico. The FBI had given them the Chevy truck to help in cataloging the numerous ghost towns and abandoned silver and smithsonite mines around Magdalena, New Mexico. He had not heard from Brandon since leaving for his assignment with Operation Alsos. Of course he had not tried to write Brandon either but promised to do so at the next break, just like he had at his last break. He was really proud to be serving as the appointed leader of the team. They were a great bunch of people in spite of their differences. There were two prominent doctoral physicists, two Army officers that were doctors in chemistry and aeronautical engineering, a Navy SEAL, two veteran Army sergeants (lifers as they called themselves), and a partridge in a pear tree. There were seven languages spoken by the various team members and very little information shared about any of their private lives aside from the operation. He had heard conflicting information about the two Army officers. One source said they were civilian physicists, the other was that they were assigned to the Army but not physicists but chemists and engineers. He finally determined that it didn't matter what they were or whom they worked for; they were still good people trying to help win the war. He was really proud to serve his country with this team as he began to finally relax, pull the blanket over his head, and quickly fall asleep.

The French tank commander and his crew and guards were up early preparing for the trip to Munster, Germany, the new camp for the captured prisoners. There were very few supplies left after sharing with the prisoners and the team would need to be resupplied by the support vehicles coming from Paris. Nate, Davis, and Cornwell were meeting informally outside the old farmhouse to decide when to continue their trip to Celle. Davis passed around a package of Camels for each of the men. "Anyone got a match?"

Nate explained, "It was learned from the interrogation of the German officers that the British troops have yet to break through the German defenses at Celle and Hanover." "The Germans hold positions three kilometers west of Celle and Hanover and the British troops are apparently close to engaging them." "What do you think we should do?" Davis was first to respond, "We can sit here and wait until it is safe or we can skirt the action by approaching Celle from the north." "According to the French tank commander the road to Bergen is in good shape and should be safe, but once we head east from Bergen we would be in farm land and no major roads." "The travel would be slower, but probably free of German troops."

Cornwell then added, "Why don't we consult with Graff? He was born and raised in this area." "He may know of a better way to get to Celle." "Our other concern will be finding provisions and petrol if we are going to be out of the 6ᵗʰ Army control area." The three men agreed that they should consult with Graff and approached him in the farmhouse where Nate asked, "Are you familiar with the area north of Celle and whether it would be wise to approach Celle from the north before the British troops have cleared the German troops from the area?" Graff answered, "A small group of vehicles moving slowly in the area would find little resistance except from the villagers." "Traveling at night would solve that problem but we would have to contend with several river crossings." "I know of several families in the area that might be of assistance or they might shoot at us depending on whether they have resigned to defeat or still fighting for the Third Reich." Nate finally added, "Our plans also depend on the arrival of our needed equipment and supplies from 6ᵗʰ Army headquarters." "We need food, petrol, trucks, and several more soldiers to move the centrifuge." "We will just have to wait for their arrival before we can decide our next move."

Two carryall trucks pulled up in front of the old farmhouse just in time for breakfast in the morning of the second day. Nate thought, *Typical Army time schedule, hurry up and wait.* The team had disposed of the prisoners with the exception of the Hitler Youth and could travel light and fast, but first things first. A "great" breakfast of dried eggs, powdered milk, and a chocolate bar with some really strong coffee with no cream or sugar. Davis thought, *Breakfast of champions and crazy sergeants.* The team now felt rested after the two-day delay that probably played well into their schedule. The British forces had captured much of the area in question around Celle and Hanover and should make the trip there much safer. Nate could not wait to get started to finish this first mission for Alsos. The centrifuge and the two physicists located at the small laboratory in Celle would be a decent finish to the team's first mission.

The two trucks with drivers and four additional personnel would be more than adequate to move the centrifuge and any other laboratory equipment in Celle and Hanover. The two lead jeeps left the old farmhouse followed by the two trucks midmorning. The small convoy evaded the pockmarked roads following the aerial bombardment and several abandoned and smoking German tanks. It made for slow travel, but progress was made. Villagers were moving further west away from Walsrode to avoid the fighting. Some pulling carts filled with all their possessions, others on bicycles and the occasional truck loaded with passengers. Some villagers had brought their prized chickens or pigs and seated holding their children or beloved pet. One lady was seen by the side of the road beside a dead cow that had been shot by either sides of the battle. She didn't care who shot her cow, but she blamed the Allies and just resigned to the fact that it was part of the war, and everyone seemed to be affected. Collateral damage in an ugly war. The lady was carrying a small baby and waved for help as the small convoy approached. Nate ordered the convoy to stop. Otto approached the lady. She was crying and asked for help in German, "My baby is hungry and my cow has been shot. Can you help me find some milk for my baby?" Otto was in the first jeep and responded, "Yes, we can help you. We have some milk." "Take my seat in my jeep and rest while I prepare the milk." Otto proceeded to the back of the first truck where the supplies had been stored. One of the soldiers in the back had heard the conversation with the lady and had begun the preparation of the powdered milk with honey before being asked. Otto asked, "I didn't know you spoke German. Where did you learn the language?" The young soldier responded, "My parents were forced to immigrate to American in 1933 as the Third Reich came to power and began forcing families with Jewish ancestry out of the country." "They taught me the language and I studied several languages in college in Indiana." Otto replied, "My family and I also left Germany for the same reason and thank you for helping mix the milk for the baby." "I hope we can talk more before we reach Celle." "Thanks for mixing the milk concoction." The Hitler Youth that had been captured on the road to Verden could not help but hear the exchange between the soldier and Otto. He was beginning to understand the plight of the displaced people caused by the Third Reich. He also began to admire this man Otto for helping the lady and her child; the suffering caused by the war needs to end and he was glad now to be in custody of the Americans. Otto then took the milk and honey to the lady now seated in the jeep and resting. "Here is the milk. It isn't warm, but your baby will love it anyway." Otto then continued, "I have put a package of dried milk in this bag along with a bottle of honey for your trip to Verden. You should find help there." "Unfortunately we cannot take you and your baby with us. We are going to Celle and it may be dangerous." "Try to stay with the other villagers as they move west toward Verden." Finally Nate had to interrupt, "Let's go, Otto. We can't wait any longer." "We must be close to Celle before dark to ensure our safety." At Nate's urging, Otto helped the lady out of the jeep and wished her well as the small convoy pulled back onto the road to Bergen. Both men were wishing there was something more they could have done to help the lady and child, but the war must be won as soon as possible to prevent incidents such as she had experienced from occurring again. The thankful woman then waved as Otto waved good-bye as the convoy moved east.

As the team approached Walsrode, they ran into several 3rd Army units headed toward Hanover. Nate, Davis, and Cornwell approached an MP directing traffic on the roads either leading southeast toward Hanover or north toward Hamburg. "Are the bridges still usable over the Aller River?" The MP responded, "No, the bridges have been destroyed by the retreating German forces." "That's why we have all this traffic. Part of the 12th Army is heading north toward Hamburg to find another route to Hanover while the 3rd Army is waiting until the engineers have built a pontoon bridge over the river." "The British have moved through Celle but still finding resistance south of Celle leading to Hanover." Graff then joined the conversation with the MP, "Is the old dirt farm road open leading east toward Celle?" The MP had no information about the road and in fact did not know it existed. Nate then asked Graff, "Do you think the road is still there and passable?" Graff responded, "It was there ten years ago. I would bet it is still there." Nate then ordered Davis to contact 3rd Army headquarters to let them know that they were headed toward Celle on an unknown road but would let them know of its condition should they want to use it to reach the area north of Hanover rather than the long circuitous route by way of Hamburg. Davis contacted headquarters and repeated the response to Nate, "You're going where and why?" "Good luck and let us know if you survive." Nate responded, "I'm so glad they are concerned for our well-being." "Let's go see if Graff is right about that road."

Graff lead the first jeep one mile north of Walsrode then

ordered Nate to turn right at the next opening in the trees. Graff admitted, "The road is still here, but not in the condition I remember." "The trees are bigger, the bushes have encroached onto the road in places, but it still looks passable." Nate then said, "Celle should be about ten miles and hopefully we will be there before dark." There was no traffic on the road and the convoy passed through beautiful farm country that looked as it did ten years ago. No war, just beautiful small farms. The main difference was that there was no traffic, no people, no cattle, no sheep or other livestock. The war had affected these farms also. There was no need for their crops, no place to sell them, no customers to buy them, and now no farmers to tend the fields.

Smoke was visible over the trees where Celle should be. It was strange that the war had such an effect. Two miles west of Celle it was peaceful and quiet while two miles east of Celle the smoldering ruins of battle stood in the way of fighting armies. As the team approached Celle, British troops were seen establishing their headquarters after pushing the Germans out of the area. The team needed to contact the local British commander to let him know they were in the area and needed his assistance in locating the small laboratory of Drs. Moth and Martek. Nate sent the two officers, Jackson and Southfield with their higher ranks to discuss the issue with the local British commander. The team had parked their small convoy in front of an old hotel that still looked habitable while the two officers spoke with the British commander. After showing their orders to the local commander and threatening to call General Eisenhower for support, the local commander relented and allowed the team to enter the part of the city where sporadic fighting was still occurring. The British commander pointed out that the city had surrendered as German troops retreated but that still some small-arms fire was slowing traffic in some areas. There had been minimal damage to the town.

In the meantime, Graff had asked the Hitler Youth if he knew where his father's laboratory was located. He told Graff that the laboratory was located in a silk factory responsible for making parachutes for the German Air Force, but he did not know the location. Graff then asked Otto to ask some of the locals where the silk factory was located. Otto approached a man walking into the small hotel where the team had parked their small convoy. "Can you direct me to the silk factory?" The man replied, "Yes, it is about eight blocks east of here. You can't miss it at the edge of town."

The two officers returned from their meeting with the British commander to find Otto, Nate, Davis, and Cornwell in conversation regarding the parachute factory. Nate explained, "The factory has been located but it is too late to start work on finding and loading the centrifuge into the trucks." "We will need to post guards around the factory tonight to make

sure the physicists and the centrifuge are not moved." Nate
then addressed Davis and Cornwell, "Davis, will you see that
guards are posted and relieved occasionally?" "Cornwell, will
you have the trucks moved to the factory to help protect
the laboratory and the two physicists from locals looking
for German sympathizers and make sure the Hitler Youth is
secure?" "Graff and Otto will go with the trucks to the factory
to contact the physicists and explain to them that they are
being held for their protection." Graff then mentioned, "At
some point we need to have Dr. Moth and his son reunited,
maybe this evening." Nate and Jackson were to see if the team
could stay in the small hotel for the night and if any food was
available.

The Silk Factory

Graff and Otto preceded the American soldiers and trucks
to the silk factory. They arrived a little early at the factory
and discovered that the factory had discontinued production
of silk and was silent except for two maintenance men too
old to be in the war. Graff asked the two workers, "Where
will we find Drs. Moth and Martek?" One of the old men
pushed his chair away from a small table where the two men
had been playing chess to spend the time. "I will show you
the laboratory of the doctors." "I don't know if the doctors
are there, but I have seen some of the laboratory technicians

today." "Please follow me." The building was massive with weaving machinery in the center and assembly tables placed along the exterior walls. The maintenance man left one building and entered another smaller building. Graff and Otto were shocked at the sight of several technicians in white coats working at benches covered by electronic equipment and glassware. A typical busy laboratory seemed out of character operating normally between battles. The centrifuge was not visible. The old maintenance man pointed to a small office behind a glass partition. "That is Dr. Moth at the desk and Dr. Martek stands behind him." Graff and Otto approached the small office to introduce themselves. "Drs. Moth and Martek, I am Dr. Otto Smitt and this is Dr. Reginald Graff." "We have come to liberate you and your staff from the Germans and to place you in protective custody by the 6th American Army." Dr. Moth recognized his doctoral student from Hamburg. "Reginald, good to see you again." "How long has it been? We have missed your joking and singing." Graff answered, "It has been ten years and yes, I have missed you too." Dr. Martek then responded, "We have been expecting the allies for some time." "We have not been contacted by the British but suspect they have other things to do." "The British had liberated the city but there are still pockets of resistance in the outskirts of the city." Dr. Graff responded, "Good to see you again, sir, not quite the circumstances I would have liked to meet you though." "We will need you to stay in the laboratory tonight before you are taken to London tomorrow." "Is there anything you will need before you leave?" Both doctors had prepared for this and had their bags packed but Dr. Martek asked the courtesy of telling his wife good-bye. Dr. Graff continued, "Of course we will transport you to your homes should you need anything, but you must stay under guard for the night." "Do you have a place here where you can sleep here?" Dr. Moth answered, "No, we always leave the laboratory in the evenings." "We have no accommodations here and would appreciate your providing us shelter for the night." Dr. Graff answered, "We should be able to provide you a place to stay with our Alsos team if the small hotel has any rooms." "For now, continue with your work as you wish. Our guards will be posted outside to make sure you are not bothered." "I will make the arrangements to take you to your homes before proceeding to the hotel." "Dr. Smitt would like to see your centrifuge while I am gone."

While Graff was gone to make the arrangements for the two doctors at the hotel, Dr. Smitt was taken to the back of the building to examine the centrifuge. Dr. Martek was really proud of the machine. "We basically assembled it with parts obtained from other laboratories and buying pieces as they became available." "It is a bit crude, but it works." Dr. Smitt then stated, "It really is quite exquisite. Isotope separation has proven to be one of the most interesting studies in physics and chemistry." Dr. Martek explained how they had assembled the device then moved it twice to keep it safe from the constant bombing raids and the occasional artillery and man-to-man battles in the area. He went on to explain that the campus at Hamburg was badly damaged before they moved the machine but the physics laboratory was undamaged.

Nate had arranged for several rooms in the almost vacant hotel for the Alsos team that had been occupied by German soldiers the previous week. The hotel manager and owner was really pleased to have the Americans stay in his hotel. The occupation had ended and he was looking forward to business as usual but knew it would take time. The Hitler Youth was placed in a room with no windows and behind a locked door. A warm place to stay with a bath and maybe some decent food was like staying at the Waldorf Astoria; the team would not complain. Graff had informed Nate about the two physicists and their needs for the night and that they wanted to be taken to their homes briefly. Nate agreed and asked if the centrifuge would be available to be removed tomorrow. Graff had not seen the centrifuge, but Otto was to examine it in his absence. Nate then mentioned, "You and Otto will be in charge of the two physicists, take a jeep and a guard to their homes, then deliver them back here before dark." Graff agreed and turned to one of the soldiers and asked him to follow him to the jeep to provide transport of the two physicists. Graff then asked,

"Are you armed in case we have unexpected company?" The soldier responded, "I will be when we reach the jeep." A short drive later the jeep pulled into the driveway at the silk factory to find the two guards watching the building and securing all the doors after all the employees had been dismissed. Graff then asked one of the guards to place the luggage of the two physicists in the truck for safekeeping. As Graff entered the laboratory, it was quiet and now vacant. He could hear voices in the back of the building and assumed it was the three men and the centrifuge he was expecting. As he entered the room where the centrifuge was located all three physicists were on their knees under the deice examining its workings. "Have you lost something, or are you just praying?" The three scientists just giggled and began to crawl from beneath the device. Otto explained, "As simple as a centrifuge is, this is the most complicated device I have ever seen." "I assume it is due to the excessive weight involved and the danger of radioactivity and poisonous gasses." Graff interrupted, "We have a jeep ready to take you to your homes and then rooms will be provided for you at the hotel." "We should leave soon before dark. The streets may not be safe if there are still a few German soldiers in the area."

Otto stayed with the centrifuge at the laboratory to begin the dismantling steps. Graff drove the jeep and was ordered to stop in front of Dr. Moth's home where he entered and returned within two minutes carrying a small case. There was apparently no Mrs. Moth. At Dr. Martek's home it took a little longer where his wife met him at the door. It was a brief good-bye and both the Marteks were in tears as he returned to the jeep. He waved and said, "I will be back as soon as possible. The Americans will take good care of me and the British will help you while I am gone."

It was dark as the jeep approached the hotel and Nate was anxiously waiting at the door like a mother hen watching over her chicks. Graff introduced the two physicists to Nate and the two captains, Jackson and Southfield. Each of the scientists were very comfortable with each other and felt relieved to being in the custody of the Americans. The café at the hotel had prepared the only food available but was supplemented by several "warm" K-rations. Not quite a meal meant for a king, but it would be a wonderful departure from their past few meals. Sergeants Davis and Cornwell were invited to join the group for the meal and then excused themselves to help feed the other men and the guards at the silk factory. Graff was holding a dish of food in his hand and explained, "Dr. Moth, you should follow me to the second floor to meet someone you know." Without questioning the reason, Dr. Broth followed Graff to the second floor. As they reached the second floor, Graff noticed the prisoner's door was open. Graff screamed that the young man had escaped. "Tell the guards to watch for him at the exits. He mustn't get away." The team was on alert and watching for the young man but no one had seen him. Graff then looked inside the room to find the Hitler Youth lying on his bed. "What's wrong? I just opened the door for a little air." Graff then entered the room with Dr. Moth. The young man jumped off his bed and grabbed his father without saying a word. Dr. Moth was crying as he clutched his son. "I thought you had been killed at Hanover." "The British news reached us yesterday that your unit had been defeated and few prisoners were taken." The young man responded, "My group was overrun by American troops and several in my squad and I escaped detection by hiding in the woods until we surrendered to this group of Americans." Dr. Moth then said, "You look wonderful. Have they taken good care of you? You look like you have lost weight." All without taking a breath or allowing his son to respond. The son finally had a chance to answer, "Yes, we had been well cared for until overrun by the American troops." "Since being captured, I have also been well cared for. Actually they saved our lives." "My unit had been wandering in the woods lost, hungry, and dodging warring groups of soldiers for days until we surrendered to the Americans." "I told my unit I wanted to continue fighting but two of older comrades wrestled me to the ground to restrain me from escaping." "Dr. Graff convinced me that the fight was futile and to work for the peace." Dr. Moth then noticed that his son wore the uniform of a Hitler Youth. "What happened that you joined the Hitler Youth?" The son responded, "My school was closed by the SS and we were instructed to join the Hitler Youth to help save the country from the invading savages from America." "I have since learned that at least these Americans are not savages, but seeking freedom for an imprisoned people." "Dr. Graff told me that he knew you from Hamburg and offered to bring me here to be with you and to go back to school and college like you and grandfather." Dr. Moth and Graff were both in tears now. Dr. Moth explained, "How can I thank you for finding my son and returning him to me?" Graff responded, "You both have fought enough in this war." "Your services are needed by the Allies to keep you and your laboratory from falling into the hands of the Russians." "Many of your colleagues have been asked to help in the effort to produce nuclear power and control nuclear fission." "Your work with heavy water and isotope separation are vital to the development of power for the free world." The young man interrupted by asking his father, "Where is Mother? I want to see her." Dr. Moth then said, "I am sorry, your mother was shot by the SS for being a Jewish sympathizer. She didn't even have a chance to explain that she was a native-born German and was not Jewish." "She had helped seven Jewish families and many children orphaned by the war escape into France where the underground helped them to immigrate to England." "Her death was another reason for me to move first to Hanover then to Celle to protect the centrifuge." "The lives of my laboratory staff was also in doubt." "Your mother and I had sent you to school thinking it would be much safer for everyone, but we could not know that the SS would become murderers of their own people."

Dr. Graff then suggested that Dr. Moth and his son Heinrich rejoin the group downstairs. As the three men entered the dining area, Dr. Moth said, "I would like to introduce myself, Dr. Wilhelm Moth, and my son Heinrich, the former Hitler Youth that you so very graciously saved and brought back to his father." "We will be forever grateful." Dr. Martek also said, "It is with heavy heart that we leave our homeland but also with joy that we join in the effort to rid the world of the men who have invented, directed, and then destroyed the Third Reich at the expense of many countries and untold innocent lives." Dr. Moth then raised his glass of some unknown fluid and toasted the Americans and the Canadian in the group. The owner or manager of the hotel had opened his wine cellar and had joined in the toast to thank the group and the British Army for freeing Celle.

Nate felt that a major battle had been won and was praising the achievements of everyone in the room. This was followed by more toasting by various members of the group until the manager of the hotel ran out of spirits and explained that it was time to go to bed, then said jokingly, "The German curfew takes effect in ten minutes."

Russians Move to Oranienburg

"How far is it to Oranienburg?" one of the team members asked Vasily. "About 125 miles and about fourteen miles north of Berlin," Vasily replied. "We will be traveling in an active war zone and very dangerous." Although Oranienburg is in our zone of occupation, it is imperative that the uranium and thorium metal is retrieved and taken to Szczecin Poland as soon as possible to complete the supplies for our super bomb 'completion.'" "The 'Mechanic' tells us that the shipment of uranium at Oranienburg is enough to complete our needed supply for several bombs." "We must leave immediately and should encounter many of our comrades in the north of Berlin as the war is coming to an end." "The 'Mechanic' tells us that the plant has been damaged by several Allied bombing raids, but the uranium metal should have survived the raids." "It will be difficult to find without a Geiger counter, but we should recognize the German markings on the containers." "It will also be necessary for us to wear our protective aprons and lead-lined gloves." "Klaus in the American Alsos headquarters tells us that the American Alsos team will not try to find the uranium and that they are searching for the metal in Toulouse and Arles." "We should find no resistance except for the few German deserters lost behind the war zone." "Stay alert and stay alive."

The Concentration Camp

"Breakfast will be served for another thirty minutes," the hotel manager announced to the team. It was 6:30 in the morning. The team's heads were feeling the "pleasures" of the previous evening. So many toasts with so much wine and spirits. The day Nate had been waiting for had finally arrived but he didn't expect it to arrive with a splitting headache. Although his head hurt, the elation he felt for discovering the centrifuge and the physicists would keep him going through the pain. The centrifuge had been located and could be loaded along with the two physicists to complete the mission he had been assigned by Operation Alsos. Two of the most prominent German physicists, their research work, and the centrifuge would be a good payoff for all the hard work and discomfort suffered by the team. Several members of the team were seated, helping themselves to the hotel manager's preserved and cherished eggs, strudel, and hot coffee when Nate joined them. He took a seat across the table from Davis and Cornwell to discuss the move of the centrifuge and the physicists. Graff and Otto joined the group to add their perspective to the move. Otto had examined the centrifuge and mentioned to Davis, "The unit is bolted to the concrete floor and is heavy, probably 750 pounds." "The unit will need to be moved upright on its base to prevent damage." "We may need to remove the canvas top of the truck to accommodate its height." Davis then responded,

"Should be easily moved by the six or seven soldiers. Will we need to build a ramp to lift the unit to the bed of the truck?" Otto responded, "No, you can back the truck to the dock in the rear of the building, should be easily slid onto the back of the truck." Davis finished his coffee and called to Cornwell to gather the soldiers and move to the silk factory in the jeeps. "Probably armed and helmets just in case we run into any resistance."

The two physicists were meeting with Graff and Otto over coffee when Nate approached. "We have learned from some British troops from the 11th Armored Division that the road to Hanover is now open but very busy with British troops and equipment moving south to Hanover and medical personnel moving north toward Bergen. Otto then asked, "Why are the medical personnel moving north away from the battle front?" Nate answered, "The British troops accidently discovered a concentration camp in Bergen. There are many prisoners needing medical care." "The troops also reported seeing hundreds of bodies lying around the camp and many more wandering aimlessly." "The camp is basically located about eight miles northwest of here in farmland." "I think they called it Bergen-Belsen concentration camp." Dr. Moth, his son, and Dr. Martek then volunteered to help with the prisoners at the camp and they were joined by Drs. Otto and Graff. Nate then said, "As much as we would all like to help at the camp, we must continue south toward Hanover and the laboratory there to complete our mission." "The soldiers mentioned that a full report on the camp would be prepared for the *Le Figaro* newspaper of Paris in the coming days." "There are numerous groups helping with the camp prisoners including the Red Cross." Davis then announced, "We are ready to leave for the silk factory if any of you would like to join us." That emptied the dining area and everyone headed for the silk factory. Nate paused before leaving to speak with the hotel manager. "We can't thank you enough for your hospitality and especially those really special eggs. We haven't seen eggs in several months now." "The wine last night had to have been the highlight of our trip." "I hope to see you again after the war." The manager then responded, "It was my pleasure. You and the British forces liberated our area and brought the peace so that we can begin rebuilding our village." Nate offered to pay for the night's stay and the great food and wine. The hotel manager responded, "We can't thank you enough to bring peace to our village and you are our guests for the evening." "There is no charge." Nate thanked the manager for his hospitality. After packing to leave, Nate left $500 under the little bell on the manager's desk with a thank you note signed by each of the team members of Operation Alsos, now with thirteen American soldiers.

The centrifuge was easily unbolted from the concrete floor and had been mounted on wooden skids when Nate finally arrived at the silk factory. Everyone was helping. Drs. Moth and Martek were helping Otto and Graff pack and load the many files concerning the research accomplished at the factory. They had been able to separate uranium 238 from uranium 235 and had produced a small amount of weapon-grade uranium. They had not produced the isotope with a nuclear bomb in mind but for the production of nuclear power to provide light to a darkened world still at war. Possibly their research and the centrifuge would increase the chances that a world war could be ended. Dr. Moth was especially happy and pleased that his son had been found and returned to him unharmed. He reasoned that somehow things were going to be better with the Third Reich's defeat.

It was with mixed feelings that Drs. Moth and Martek left Celle for Hanover. They had accomplished much in isotope separation and heavy water production, but they missed the comradery with the laboratory staff. The staff had to be released in Celle but could possibly join other laboratory staff in Hanover after the war. Before the team left Celle, Nate wanted to meet with Graff and Otto concerning Dr. Moth's son. "What can be done with the young man?" The three men were concerned that they could not take the young man with them but even more concerned with what could happen by leaving him behind. Graff finally said, "Let me discuss the problem with his father." "There may be relatives where the young man could stay or possibly return him to the school where the SS had interrupted his studies." Nate and Otto agreed to have Graff discuss the situation with Dr. Moth where he was seated in his laboratory office reminiscing the results of the many years of work with Dr. Martek and the laboratory staff. Graff entered the office and asked, "What can be done with your son? We cannot take him with us." Dr. Moth had also been considering the issue and said, "His grandmother still lives in a suburb of Hamburg and could use the company." "If we can find a way for him to reach Hamburg he will be safe and completely out of the war." Graff then volunteered. "I will drive him there if you will accompany us." "It will give us a chance to talk about the good times before the war." "I also want to discuss a couple of problems I encountered in my studies of heavy water." Graff was pleased to discuss any problem concerning physics and the chance to drive the young man and his father to Hamburg.

Nate was not pleased with the plan for Graff to be out of his protection; one of the captured physicists loose and his Hitler Youth son out driving around in an open jeep in recently liberated territory was not a reassuring picture. "You are insane, but I like the idea." "If you let a well-armed Sergeant Davis accompany you, I think it might work." Graff then said, "I promise not to tell Major Powers. He would probably have us both shot." Nate then said, "We will wait for you, at the University of Hanover where we will be dismantling the Hanover laboratory." "Make it quick. We must leave Hanover in two days."

The Gottfried Wilhelm Leibniz University Hanover, founded in 1831, located in Lower Saxony, Germany, was not quite what the team expected. The German Army was in retreat and surrendering in masses. The beautiful campus with panoramic green lawns and large trees had become a barbed wire city to accommodate the many German soldiers resigned to defeat and surrendering to the Allies. The buildings were being used as barracks for the many soldiers needed to protect and contain the prisoners of war. In the absence of Dr. Moth, Dr. Martek led the team to what used to be the laboratory where the centrifuge and many of their studies had been completed. Much of the university staff still remained to help with the prisoners and to preserve the campus from complete destruction. As Dr. Martek entered the laboratory, he was greeted by several of the remaining laboratory staff. "How have you been? We have really missed you and Dr. Moth." Then Dr. Martek asked, "It is good to see you again also. What have you been doing in our absence?" A married couple from Spain, who had joined the laboratory staff recently, said, "We couldn't do much." "The Gestapo, Section IIIc, had requested information concerning the laboratory, which took several weeks to accomplish. The letter was addressed to you and read:

'As a notable pupil of Heisenberg I request that you send my office a short survey report on the present state of theoretical physics, how it is sponsored by government and political departments, and how to effect its possible application to so-called war research. Moreover we are in general also interested in your views on so-called German physics. I would be grateful if you would grant my wish as soon as possible and greet you with 'Heil Hitler!' (Name unreadable) SS----Lt. Colonel' 1 (3)

The SS had ordered them to gather all research material and prepare it for shipping along with any chemicals and raw minerals that remain of value. One of the Spanish laboratory technicians then said, "The operative word was 'value,' which we interpreted rather loosely." "The reams of statistics, preliminary diagrams, and chemicals were all packed for shipping separately from the 'valuable' material." The other Spanish technician then added, "The SS proceeded to take the material to an undisclosed location while your research results and the uranium metal has been saved for your use and packed away in the basement for safekeeping." One of the other staff asked, "Where is Dr. Moth?" Dr. Martek then answered, "He was reunited with his son and they are on their way to Hamburg to leave his son with his grandmother." "He will join us here on his return." Dr. Martek then asked the staff, "Will you show these men where the packed research materials and the uranium metal has been stored?" "They will deliver Dr. Moth and me along with the material to another location to help in the effort to end the war." Nate and Sergeant Cornwell then followed the pair of Spanish technicians to the basement. While they were out of earshot, one of the other technicians told Dr. Martek that the Spanish couple appeared to be Russian spies. They were observed photographing all of Dr. Harteck's research papers, inventorying all chemicals and procedures involved with the heavy water project and the centrifuge results. The Spanish couple were also observed leaving the laboratory frequently to meet with someone at the café of the Kastens Hotel. Dr. Martek then said, "Thanks for the information and please forget our conversation." "We will deal with the spies."

As Nate returned followed by several soldiers moving the packaged materials, Dr. Martek asked, "Are there places where we could spend the night close to the university?" The technicians agreed in unison, "Yes, the Kastens is one of the best and the German soldiers stayed elsewhere." Dr. Martek then wanted to confer with Otto and Nate. "Should we stay at the Kastens, and if so, should I invite the laboratory staff to join us for dinner or a drink?" It was one of those questions that Nate loved to hear and seldom refused. "Sure, but just two drinks. I am still nursing a headache from last night and I shot our budget in Celle." "Hopefully Drs. Graff and Moth will rejoin us during the night or tomorrow morning." Dr. Martek approached Nate about the two Russian spies, "I have learned from our staff that the two Spanish laboratory assistants are suspected of being Russian spies." "They were observed photographing our research work and shipping samples of our chemistry elsewhere." "They were also observed meeting regularly with someone at the café at the Kastens Hotel." Nate then responded, "What do you think we should do about the spies?" Dr. Martek then reasoned, "Many German soldiers are being held prisoner on the campus. Why don't we have them incarcerated with the prisoners and have them questioned by the authorities?" "We don't have proof that they are spies, but the authorities can determine whether they are or not and what to do with them." "If nothing else happens, they won't be able to communicate with other spies or their offices." Nate agreed and asked Jackson to alert the prison camp to have them arrested and questioned. In the meantime, the team finished the day with a happy reunion party at the Kastens Hotel café. Just like clockwork, Drs. Moth and Graff rejoined them later that evening and were prepared to leave for Paris to finish their first Alsos mission.

Chapter 10

Alsos Headquarters, Paris

Sergeant Martinez was frustrated. He was tired of waiting for the 6th and 12th Armies to finally push the German Army out of France and start the search for the uranium supplies reported to be in Strasbourg, Arles, and Toulouse. Blake and Sergeant Martinez had been assigned to work with another Army group, but they had not been told which Army group yet. All they knew was that there were nine railcars sitting somewhere in Toulouse full of uranium that needed to be found and delivered to Marseille for shipment to England and ultimately to the United States. The new Army assignment would have the responsibility of the central and southern portions of France and move into the southern and eastern portion of Germany and possibly Austria. According to the Yalta Agreement between the "Big Three" of Roosevelt, Stalin, and Churchill, the German-occupied countries including Germany were to be divided equally into three zones of responsibility and reciprocity. Russian territories were generally the eastern zone while the British, the Americans, and the French would equally share the rest. Unfortunately, the eastern and southern parts of Germany were generally in the Russian sector of responsibility after the war and it would be really tricky working around the German and Russian armies to find Dr. Werner Heisenberg. Apparently there were Alsos targets in both the Russian and French sectors that would require Blake's team to work very inconspicuously and quietly while intruding into French and Russian occupational zones. Blake and Martinez were looking forward to leaving Paris and working with John and Dino in Toulouse. John had been working with the Italian underground to locate a significant load of 1,400 tons of uranium ore from the Belgium Congo and now somewhere in Arles or Marseille. John and Dino's Alsos team was very successful on their first mission and would need the support and help of the Italian underground in locating and moving the uranium ore back to Marseille for shipment to London. The three eminent Italian physicists had been successfully moved out of Venice and to Tunis awaiting transportation to London. Following the short "vacation" of the Italy team in London, they were to arrive by air in Paris sometime during the night to join Blake and Martinez to find and recover the uranium in southern France.

Major Powers had moved the Alsos headquarters from London

to Paris to be closer to the action and was now directing the various Alsos teams searching for the elusive nuclear physicists, their laboratories, and the much needed uranium. One of his first tasks was to question Blake about his adopted assistant, Sergeant Martinez. Major Powers asked, "Who is this character Martinez? You were supposed to operate as a confidential representative of the United States Army and not a representative of the Mexican Mafia." "Where did he come from and how did you find him?" Blake finally had a chance to speak. "Well, he was given to me by a British colonel at Normandy and he then volunteered to help rather than drive the tank that he had sunk off the beach at Normandy." "He was assigned to me along with a jeep directly off the beachhead." "We were thrown together by accident and I would still be hiding behind bunkers just off the beach if he hadn't helped me move through the various groups fighting their way toward Paris." "He has been helpful in many ways." "First, he speaks fluent French and can read and understand the very confusing road signs." "He has been able to supply many needed things, some of them may have been 'borrowed' without permission, but if we had waited until we received permission around here, the war would be over before we could get to work." Major Powers then asked, "I thought he was a corporal but apparently he promoted himself to sergeant without authority." Blake, in his defense, then said, "I did that. He was having trouble directing other military personnel who would not listen to or obey a corporal." Major Powers finally gave up. It was a lost cause to argue with the success that Blake and Martinez had achieved but he would have to process several piles of paper to assign Martinez to the team and officially promote him to sergeant.

Major Powers had reassigned the Italian team to help Blake's team in southern France and would be responsible to another Army group where most of the hostilities were small groups of German soldiers trapped behind the main battle lines and the French underground. Surprisingly, the French underground was fighting both the Germans and the French armies to gain control of small regions of southern France where the absence of authority and police made for easy theft. Major Powers was also awaiting the arrival of Nate and his team from Hanover where they had secured two of the most important physicists, their laboratories, their research, and of course, their elusive centrifuge that had been moved three times before the team finally found it in Celle. It had been a successful mission and Major Powers had arranged for the team to relax a few days before starting another mission. The two German scientists would join the three Italian physicists in Tunis while the centrifuge would be transported to the United States along with the research results from Drs. Moth and Martek.

Nate's team finally arrived in Paris at 1500 hours following the 850-mile trip from Hanover with overnight stops in Duisburg,

Germany, and Namur, Belgium. The trip was perilous, not from battles with German soldiers but from Allied traffic moving in the opposite direction toward Berlin. The roads were thick with all sorts of vehicles and personnel. Most of the vehicles moving south were much larger than the leading jeep of Nate's team and would require moving off the road to keep from being pushed into the ditch by an oncoming tank or truck. There had been near-misses of the jeeps and one truck actually scraped the side of the team's truck carrying the laboratory equipment and the centrifuge. The tanks were always given a wide birth and no contact was ever made with them, thank goodness. It was not a "fun" trip and Nate's team was ready for some refreshments and a few drinks to calm their nerves. Major Powers met Nate at the door of the small hotel where they would be staying for a few days before departing for another assignment. Blake had joined the major to greet Nate, "Whasss uppp?" Nate responded, "Nutttin much, but you could start something by buying me a few drinks." Major Powers was at a loss at what he could add to their conversation except to warn the two friends that they were on a tight budget. Major Powers then excused himself, but not before inviting the two team leaders to dinner to include their teams and any of the military personnel helping the teams. Nate and Blake were headed toward a small café on the front sidewalk of the hotel when Nate noticed the headlines on the Paris newspaper, *Le Figaro*: "Bergen-Belsen Concentration

Camp Discovered at Bergen, Germany." Nate grabbed a copy but continued to walk with Blake to the café. He could not read the details of the camp's discovery to Blake but did want to have Graff translate them for him and apologize for having to leave Celle without assisting the camp survivors. The story must be important to be on the front page of the Paris paper, but he wasn't sure he wanted to read the details.

Nate and Blake had a lot to catch up on. They had not seen each other for over four months as they departed the London Alsos headquarters for their separate assignments. Nate apologized for not writing but then remembered that Blake had not bothered to write either. Nate then asked, "How is Vivian? Has she recovered from losing her best friend and her husband?" Blake responded, "Yes, she has recovered but still mad at me and the luncheon at the Water Canyon Lodge where we had postponing our wedding again for the um-teenth time. I have written to her regularly and she responded and even asked about you once." The waiter brought another round of their favorite elixir, Crown Royal, just as Davis, Cornwell, and Martinez approached the sidewalk café. Nate asked, "What have you guys been doing and where have you been?" Sergeant Martinez spoke for the three men, "Getting acquainted over a couple of beers and watching the pretty girls on their bicycles." Blake interrupted, "Have you been told about the dinner tonight here at the hotel? Major Powers is buying." "Check with the other men that helped move the centrifuge and driving the trucks. They are invited too." Davis and Cornwell said they would after they had another beer that Nate had promised. For the next hour, the five men swapped lies about the missions they had accomplished, the girls they had known, and how hot it was in Texas in August. Finally, Nate excused himself to check into his room and to find Graff to translate the newspaper for him. "I'll see you guys this evening. There is something I have to do."

Graff was tired and did not want to translate the newspaper for Nate. He also knew he would not like the story. Reluctant as he was, Graff read the paper for Nate, who was intermittently sick and furious. The paper described the location of the Bergen-Belsen Concentration Camp as five miles northwest of Calle in a beautiful and remote farming country. That was the only pleasant part of the article. It went on to describe what the British 11th Armored Division had accidentally found as inhumane, barbaric, and the most despicable wartime crime they had ever seen. At first entry, there were thirteen thousand dead and unburied bodies lying around the camp and hundreds more wandering aimlessly most without clothing. The German officer assigned to manage the camp had released most of the SS soldiers and guards before the Allied troops arrived at the camp leaving only a skeleton crew to care for the 4,500 dying prisoners and another 14,000 prisoners in various stages of starvation. According to the camp records, twenty thousand Russian soldiers had been imprisoned and killed there over the three-year period since it was built. Another thirty-five thousand died of typhus and fifty thousand killed who were mainly Jewish. The camp records listed those killed as Jewish, Czechs, Poles, anti-Nazi Christians, homosexuals, Italians, gypsies and Turks. The article went on to say that Bergen-Belsen was one of several reported by advancing Allied forces. It was estimated that there were twenty-five such camps that had been discovered by Allied forces as they liberated areas in the countries occupied by the Germans. Graff had enough and excused himself from Nate's room leaving Nate to try to make sense of what he had just heard. What sort of system of government allowed such cruelty to its own citizens, opposing the regime or not? Even conscripting young children to fight alongside old men. Nate was glad that Graff had left; he was either going to be sick or energized to finally end the rule of such a corrupt government. He finally settled for a quick cold shower before dressing for Major Powers's dinner.

The evening was a pleasant departure from the past few months living off the land and K-rations only supplemented with C-rations for more formal dining. There were no cooks or anything to cook most of the time, but many of the liberated villages and farmers had wonderful delicacies like homemade cheeses and local wines and beers that they generously shared while not knowing where their next meal would be found. There had been short breaks in activity, but there was always the shortage of food, gasoline, and especially clean underwear. The destruction of the cities and villages they had visited or drove through had been the most depressing and miserable part of their missions and yet the most encouraging as life and rebuilding continues in spite of the war. There had been a few highlights like the finding of Dr. Moth's son in a Hitler Youth uniform and returning him to his father to continue his war out of uniform and with his grandmother in suburban Hamburg. They had met wonderful people who seemed unaffected by the war around them and continued to live through the horrors of war that effected many of their neighbors and loved ones. The dinner was pleasant with comrades enjoying each other's simple presence without regard of religion, color of skin, sexual preference, and especially their political views or rank in life. It seems that the only time freedom is appreciated is the time when it is replaced by something else and it is lost.

These members of the Alsos missions were not close friends or related in any way except through a common goal of helping the United States build the first atomic bomb instead of Germany and bring peace back into the lives of the oppressed and countless people worldwide.

About halfway through dinner, the team of Dino and John appeared in the café. Most members of the three teams had not met but it was obvious they were immediate friends. Their spirits were being refreshed by other spirits, mainly beer and wine, but other personal spirits too. The comradery of the various teams spread to each team and even to Major Powers, who was trying to remain aloof and officer-like even though most of the team members were physicists, scientists, journalists, lawyers, and just altogether good people and civilians in military uniform. Major Powers interrupted the noisy fellowship with a request. "I would like to propose a toast." "To the people who make a difference in winning this war, to the Alsos mission teams." "Raise your glasses to the best nonsoldiers in the Army and those of you who are actually military personnel." Major Powers had another announcement. "One more drink and off to bed." "You are scheduled to leave Paris at 0700 in the morning after a short briefing at 0630." "Get some sleep and we will see you in the morning." Of course, that order was for the other two teams. Nate's team was taking a few days of well-deserved vacation to rest before their next assignment.

Seven Carloads of Uranium

It was a horrible time to leave Paris. Spring chases the cold and gloomy winter days out of the "City of Lights" and ushers in sidewalk cafés, blooming everything and lovers picnicking in the city parks. Blake had almost forgotten the war while in

Paris, but outside of the city he was again reminded that the war was far from over. The trip south toward Toulouse would be a long drive through previously German-occupied towns and villages that would show the scars of the battles to drive the Third Reich out of France. The area had been liberated by the Allied forces, but the work had just begun to repair and rebuild and there were still pockets of resistance of soldiers lost from their battle groups or deserters as they were driven out of France.

Blake and Martinez had met with John and Dino to discuss the two objectives of their mission. The first would be the nine carloads of uranium ore either in railcars in Toulouse or stored somewhere. The second objective was to recover the 1,400 tons of uranium ore that was shipped from the Belgium Congo to Genoa, Italy, then moved to the port of Marseille, possibly shipped to Arles and now misplaced. Blake was curious. "How do you misplace 1,400 tons of anything much less a material that is highly radioactive?" Dino had a quick answer, "You call it yellow dirt and the underground will steal it thinking it is gold dust." "The area where we will be going has a history of a strong French underground and with the French Army busy in Germany, they are sure to be a powerful force." "We may be able to work with them through the Italian underground that had helped us in Italy." Blake then asked, "Do you think the Italian underground will help us in

France? Toulouse is 340 miles from the Italian border." John answered, "They helped me from the Italian border to Marseille and I know they will help in Toulouse if asked." "We were tracking the ship from Genoa to Marseille when we lost track of the shipment as it was unloaded from the ship." "I was able to develop a good relationship with the leader of the underground and Dino worked well with another part of the Italian underground in Venice."

The teams heading to Toulouse included Blake, Martinez, John, Dino, two new physicists to Operation Alsos from Los Alamos and four soldiers to help with security. The combined teams were equipped with three jeeps, two large five-ton trucks and were well equipped with arms that were concealed except for the firearms hanging from their belts. All personnel carried a Colt .45 and the soldiers were equipped with a new M1 rifle and a Thompson submachine gun each.

The plan was to drive straight through to Clermont-Ferrand the first day, about 240 miles with a stop in Orleans to follow a lead from Dr. Graff on a rare earth minerals—manufacturing company that supposedly stored several tons of thorium and uranium and had been abandoned as the Germans retreated. The company was a division of the German company Auer-Gesellschaft. As the teams approached the town of Artenay about five miles from Orleans, they came upon a downed tree across the road. Blake stopped two hundred yards from the tree, anticipating an ambush. Everyone was tense and expecting armed Germans to appear from the trees. Blake asked Martinez and one of the soldiers now armed with Thompson submachine guns to scout the woods on either side of the road. "Be careful. We don't know who might be prepared for an ambush. It could be locals thinking a German patrol is approaching." Just as the two soldiers approached the tree, the bray of a mule was heard in the underbrush. Martinez then said, "What the hell is that?" The bray of the mule was followed by a male voice cussing in French. Martinez spoke French, but he could not tell what the old man was mad about. Suddenly, the mule jumped out into the road and began to squeal and kick its feet into the air hoping to hit the old man yielding a switch. The old man had tied the mule to the tree stump hidden in the brush and was attempting to move the tree from the road. Martinez then asked, "Does the old man need help with the tree?" One of the new Alsos physicists, Dr. James Roemer, walked up to the tree and spoke to the old man in French. "Would you like us to shoot your mule?" The old man was surprised to see the three soldiers by the tree and exclaimed, "Please, rid the world of this foul animal." The physicists then asked, "What would you like us to do?" "Should we attach one of the jeeps to the rope to help move the tree?" The old man responded, "Yes, yes, I am needing the wood to repair my building." Roemer relayed the message to Blake, who attached a rope to the tree and began to pull the tree out of the road while the mule acted like he was actually helping. The old man directed Blake, Martinez, and Roemer up the road about one hundred yards to a small road leading into the trees to his left. The dense forest finally yielded to a small opening where the old man had built a modest frame and rock house next to a small vegetable garden and surrounded by massive cork oak trees. As Blake, Martinez, and Roemer approached the farmhouse, an old woman came to the door waving a shotgun in Blake's direction. The old man disarmed his wife and explained that the Americans had helped him move the tree. Finally the old woman smiled and waved a large pan and motioned for the three men to come into their home. She failed to see the rest of the team still parked on the main road. The old man told the three men to bring the team around to the back of the house where they could park their vehicles and join him at a large wooden table under massive cork oak trees. The table was a heavy piece of hardwood and was undamaged while the small building next to the table and behind the farmhouse had partially collapsed. The old man explained that a recent bombing attack on the factory behind their home had damaged his building by a stray bomb but had destroyed the factory. He went on to say that he would not miss the noisy factory with its continual noisy machines. As the rest of the Alsos team joined Blake, Martinez, and Roemer, the old lady of the house brought mugs of a "dark fluid" for the three men. She cussed the old man over the size of the growing group and returned to the house for more mugs and "dark fluid." Roemer and the other physicist, Dr. Brian Jenkins, who also spoke French, began to ask the old man about the factory and the damage to his small building. Jenkins asked, "Do you have enough wood to repair your building?" "Could we help you find more wood or nails?" The old man was surprised that the Americans had volunteered to help repair his building and answered, "Yes, I will need three more trees the size of the dead one I found by the road." "I have nails and a saw and axe to cut the planks from the trees." The old lady had returned to the table with more mugs and "dark fluid" but had not changed her disposition. She cussed the old man again and disappeared into their home. Roemer and Jenkins then introduced all the team and the old man said his name was Andre Guston, a retired brick layer from Orleans while his wife had farmed in the area all her life. The old man explained the "dark fluid" by saying his wife had always made wine while he preferred beer and they had compromised on the concoction before them in the mugs. Blake had ventured a taste before anyone else and had exclaimed, "This is really good, reminds me of hard apple cider, a little sweet and a little bitter and a strong aftertaste." The rest of the team then ventured to try the "dark fluid." Everyone seemed to like it, or at least politely pretended to like it. Andre had gone into the house and returned with a large wheel of cheese and placed it in the center of the table. Blake then asked Martinez to forward a message to their hosts. "Tell Andre thanks and that we will help with the repair of his building."

Everyone was enjoying the break in the trip to Orleans and especially the "dark fluid" with its faint fruity taste with a heavy aftertaste and kick. Blake had asked two of the soldiers to help him fell three more dead trees for the repair of the building and had ask John and Dino to take the other two soldiers to begin clearing the debris from the building before they could begin the rebuilding process. Andre, James, and Brian were seated talking about the factory behind the farmhouse. Andre described the noise as an "airplane" that did not move. The Germans had abandoned the factory just after the Allied forces landed at Normandy and were in the process of rebuilding the factory following the bombing raid that damaged his building. James and Brian were very interested in the factory and asked Andre to take them to the site. James had explained to Brian that recent information had disclosed that a factory that made jet engines was in operation but the factory was thought to be further east and north in Germany. "This could be the factory reported to be building jet engines."

"The sound would be similar to the sound of an airplane."

The Factory

Andre led the two physicists through the thick forest to a hill overlooking a grassy valley surrounded by large cork oak trees that concealed the factory. A tall wire fence surrounded the large concrete building in the center of the enclosure. There was one access gate and a narrow road leading through the forest to the road to Orleans. The access road was hardly visible from the Orleans road and had been damaged in the bombing raid. Two walls of building were still standing and the roof had collapsed around a pile of debris and some equipment. Andre led the two physicists to the front of the factory to find a heavy iron gate and locked. Andre then said, "Follow me. I know an area of the fence where we can enter." The three men then passed through a hole under the fence where a bomb had blasted out several yards of dirt from under the fence but leaving the fence undamaged. The three men began to climb over the piles of debris that was the front of the factory. Recent rains had made the debris slick and in some areas had collapsed onto the concrete floor. James found a file cabinet covered with part of the roof and asked Brian for assistance. "Hopefully, we will find a paper trail to explain the purpose of the factory." "I also spotted several pieces of equipment in the corner that might help explain their production." Brian noted, "I'm smelling something dead under all this debris. I hope it isn't human." Andre then added, "That's the smell that we always noted before the bombing raid." James had cleared the debris from the file cabinet and was starting his search through the records while Brian and Andre continued working their way to the back of the building toward the equipment. Andre had found piles of glassware and containers of chemicals but did not want to examine them closely. Before Brian could reach the equipment in the back of the room, James exclaimed, "Don't touch anything and let's get out of here." "I think this is a factory to produce biological gasses to be used in warfare." Brian agreed and added, "I'm not sure about most of the equipment but I can see a small laboratory centrifuge, incubators, glassware, and tanks of compressed gasses." "The noise that Andre heard was probably mixing equipment or the centrifuge." Satisfied with their search of the factory, the three men returned to the farmhouse to rejoin the other team members.

Blake was listening to the three men explain what they had found at the factory while they washed everything they had worn and showered in the back yard with homemade soap. Blake then explained, "We must radio Paris for instructions. I'm sure the information will be important to the leaders of the 6th and 12th Armies." "They had been alerted that the Germans may have biological gasses to be used at the landing of Allied troops at Normandy." "Headquarters will probably send a team to verify your findings and properly dispose of the factory and its contents." "Let Andre know that he can expect another team of soldiers to arrive tomorrow to dispose of the factory and the noxious orders." "In the meantime, we can have Andre's building repaired and leave for Orleans tomorrow evening." After Brian had interpreted Blake's conversation too, he joined Dino in clearing the building of unusable materials and Blake began helping John cut the logs from the four dead fallen trees. Brian and James were studying the building and decided that it would need a new roof. They then realized that the big metal gate at the factory would make a perfect roof and asked two of the soldiers to take them to the factory in one of the trucks to disassemble the gate and move it to the building site. The old woman came out of her house and was shocked by all the activity. The group had hardly touched the cheese but the "dark fluid" had evaporated. Andre and several men were clearing the building of broken timbers, another group of men were cutting new timbers from the four trees, and the last group of men were leaving in a big truck going somewhere. She couldn't help but notice the old mule seemed to be pouting, or at least sorry not to be part of the activity. It was work that the mule had done in the past and probably felt left out. She was actually feeling sorry for the mangy old mule that had caused them so much grief while working around the farm. She decided to give him some extra oats to make him feel better.

Things were progressing well. The gate had been "taken" for the roof, the logs had been cut, and the building site had been cleared of broken timbers. Andre was working alongside John and Dino when he heard his wife bang something metal to sound like a bell. Curious, Andre went to see what had created the noise. Andre's wife had prepared more "dark fluid," cheese, and hot bread for the groups and had announced the meal with the banging of a large metal spoon against the big pan that she had motioned to Blake, Martinez, and Roemer at the front door. The construction quickly stopped and everyone gathered around the table just as the sun was disappearing behind the horizon in bright pink hews. It had been several hours of hard work that everyone seemed to enjoy. The conversation around the table was light-hearted and in three different languages including Italian and Martinez didn't dare introduce Spanish into the mix. That didn't stop the intermittent laughter between mouthfuls of "dark fluid" and fresh bread. Even the mule had announced his approval with several elongated brays. Blake then thought, *Good thing that mule is tied to the fence or he would be trying to steal some of my "dark fluid" and fresh bread.* Blake then discovered that the "dark fluid" had an unexpected effect on his equilibrium and he fell off his stool while laughing at Dino telling a joke in Italian. He didn't even know why he was laughing since he didn't understand the Italian language; it just sounded funny. He then thought, *Maybe they are not laughing at the joke but at me for falling off my stool.* Either way, he was enjoying the "dark fluid" and laughter. Everyone was enjoying the evening but especially the "dark fluid" when the soldier operating the radio approached Blake, who was still sitting on the ground and giggling uncontrollably. "Major Powers said to wait for the disposal team that should arrive by tomorrow evening and to direct them to the factory before proceeding to Orleans." Blake sobered enough to recognize the name "Major Powers" and the instructions he had given to the soldier. Blake then responded, "That worked out well. We can stay through tomorrow just like we had planned." Andre or his wife had not told anyone about the ingredients of the "dark fluid" but then again no one cared after the evening of merriment. Then Andre noted, "Maybe we shouldn't tell them."

The next morning found the team sleeping in various places that seemed more convenient than by design. The "dark fluid" had not kept anyone awake. In fact the opposite was more accurate with team members still asleep well past sunrise. Some were sleeping in the grass under the huge cork oak trees by the table, a couple under the table, others were in sleeping bags in the truck, while some found the jeep seats more comfortable. Andre and his wife retreated to the house and apparently were not affected by the "dark fluid." Early morning farm sounds permeated the fresh spring air. A rooster or two began their wake-up tunes while the old mule started his braying for early morning oats for breakfast. The sound of a cow bell also meant that Andre would be up to do the milking. Blake opened his eyes slowly, not so much from the bright light but from the pain involved in moving his eyelids. He had fallen off his stool early in the party and decided to stay seated on the ground for safety's sake then fell asleep under the tree and Martinez had joined him by leaning against one of the big trees. John and Dino were also stirring at the smell of something cooking in the farmhouse. The old woman came to the back door and was surprised to see the mass of humanity huddled in the grass under the trees, in the jeeps, in bedrolls and not up working. Andre had retreated to the barn to milk the cow and to gather a few eggs when he heard his wife banging the pan with the metal spoon again. That meant only one thing: she had cooked something and it was ready to eat and it was time to get to work on the building. Andre exclaimed to his wife, "Let the poor boys sleep. They are not used to your drink." The old woman would have none of that. "It's time to get to work. Get them up. I will bring out the food."

Work on the building started immediately after Andre's wife took the remaining food off the table. She had explained, "Now get to work. You have had enough fun and rest." Blake was really pleased with the progress of repairing the old building and announced, "We should be done by midafternoon. Is there anything you need us to do before we leave?" Blake regretted his dumb question before he had finished asking. Roemer interpreted for Blake as Andre's wife responded, "Yes. Cut some firewood. We will need it for cooking." She was pointing at the two axes leaning against a tree. Andre apologized for his wife but the suggestion had been made and now Blake had to comply with her wish. Two of the younger soldiers volunteered to cut the wood while the rest of the team continued work on the old building.

Just like clockwork, a demolition team from Paris arrived as planned. Andre agreed to take the demolition team to the factory while Blake readied the team to depart for Orleans. John and Dino were finished with the repair work of the building and had asked Andre for more "dark fluid" to take with them to Orleans. Andre's wife had already prepared a "package" for their trip and handed it to John and gave him a huge hug while Andre stood helplessly beside Dino wondering who she would hug next. For a small old lady, she had arms the size of Dino's thighs and a crushing handshake. Blake was watching the little departure party and hoping he wasn't on her list to hug, but he was wrong. She also had a package for Blake and another monster hug that squeezed the breath out of him.

The team finally left Andre and his wonderful wife after much chatter in three languages, handshakes, and more hugs. Blake was thinking, *These are the people that wars are fought over. All parties in a war covet these people. The politicians and the soldiers just do the fighting to be able to count these people as "citizens."* They reminded him of his grandparents and their constant battle with Mother Nature to scratch out a living from the dirt in the panhandle of Oklahoma. Never met a stranger or had an enemy; just tried to survive and enjoy what they had." It was time to leave for Orleans. Blake's team had directed the demolition team to the site of the factory; the building had been repaired and everyone had been hugged or squeezed by both Andre and his wife. Blake still had trouble making his eyelids work properly after the wonderful evening with the "dark fluid" and wonderful company. The war must go on.

As the team approached Orleans, it didn't take long to find the German company Auer-Gesellschaft. It was located in the outskirts of Orleans within three miles of the farmhouse where they had spent the night. This was the factory that Dr. Graff had indicated was possibly a supplier of uranium and thorium metals and possibly some heavy water. Like the biological factory, the plant of Auer-Gesellschaft had been bombed but not totally destroyed. The two physicists, James and Brian, armed themselves with a Geiger counter each and began the search through the rubble of the warehouse. There were barrels, drums, and sacks of various chemicals in stacks and some were damaged and opened, revealing their contents. Rain had created pools of murky fluid that would require another trip for a disposal team. James skirted one of the larger pools of stagnant water when his Geiger counter went crazy. "Good news. I've found the uranium." The Geiger counter had been checked again and Brian followed James to check the stack of metal barrels that had activated the Geiger counter. The barrels were not the normal container for uranium oxide but were in larger barrels with the German swastika and "AOL," Arles Olive Cannery, and another label featuring a skull and crossbones. "There must be two hundred barrels here. We will need to contact Paris to arrange transport of the barrels to Marseille." Blake was on the radio with Major Powers describing their find at the plant. "Should we attempt to move any of the uranium or should we leave two guards here to make sure none of the materials disappear or contaminate anyone who might wander into the building?" Major Powers responded, "You have done your job. You have located the uranium." "You can leave the move of the material to the demolition team and continue your trip to Toulouse." "Check to see if there is any other material we might need and call me back tonight." "We will wait for your report before sending out the demolition team in case there is more material to recover." Blake then answered, "We will check for other material and call you back tonight before we leave to find a place to spend the night." Major Powers then added, "Good work. Thank everyone for me and buy them a beer tonight."

Chapter 11

John and Dino Ordered to

Fly to Marseille

The uranium oxide found in Orleans at the Auer-Gesellschaft plant would be enough material for the Germans to build four atomic bombs plus muchneeded thorium and pure carbon. The Alsos teams' locating and retrieving the supplies made it possible for the United States to build the first atomic bomb and prevented the Russians from gaining materials that they were needing for their "super bomb" project.

Major Powers was pleased with the team's results and had ordered the four soldiers to stay at the plant to secure the plant and await the arrival of the demolition team. Major Powers also ordered John and Dino to catch a flight from the grass field at St. Jean de Braye two miles east of Orleans at dawn to be flown to Marseille and to meet with the Italian underground. Their mission was to work with the Italian underground in an attempt to find the 1,400 tons of uranium ore off-loaded from the Belgium ship at Marseille. Blake and Martinez were ordered to continue to Toulouse with the two physicists and would be joined by a T-Force team of four new soldiers that would arrive with the demolition team.

The team had found a small unoccupied house in the area of the German company where they decided to spend the night. It would be a short night with the departure of John and Dino before dawn at the grass airfield, the arrival of the demolition team, and the T-Force of four new soldiers to travel with Blake's team to Toulouse. Blake finally said, "I'm tired of just thinking about the move to Toulouse." "The 'package' that Andre's wife gave me will be appreciated tonight." Martinez and the two physicists were without 'packages' and would have to live on K-rations again and didn't like the idea. Martinez was about to leave the small house in search for something better to eat and drink when he was stopped by James, one of the physicists. "Take me with you. I can speak French too and I can keep you stay out of trouble." Martinez agreed, "Thanks. I probably will need the help." James then countered, "We should let Blake know that we are leaving. I would hate for him to worry about us."

Spring in Orleans was just like Paris—warm days and cool

nights with one major difference: it had been exposed to more bombing and destruction. The streets were still passable but just barely, with piles of debris pushed to the sidewalks to allow passage of construction equipment. The people were at work on individual homes and businesses, but the task was daunting. As Martinez and James crossed the river bridge leading to the center of town, the towers of the Orleans Cathedral Sainte-Croix were visible but something was missing. The bombing or artillery had destroyed the three massive towering steeples but left the base towers damaged but still standing. Martinez then asked James, "Isn't that the area where Joan de Arc, 'The Maid of Orleans,' was tried, convicted, and burned at the stake in 1431?" James answered, "I'm not sure whether she was tried and convicted there, but I think that she was burned at the stake in Orleans on that date." Martinez then said, "I would like to see the old cathedral and if it has been damaged beyond repair." As the two men neared the cathedral, James recounted more history, "Construction began on the original church building in 1287 and it was destroyed during the Protestant Revolt in 1568." "Henry IV ordered it to be rebuilt in 1601." "It is about the same size as Notre Dame de Paris." "In fact the first church built here was during the time of the Roman Empire." Martinez then responded, "That's amazing. The oldest buildings in my hometown, El Paso, Texas, date back to the Spanish explorer Onate on his way to Santa Fe, New Mexico, in 1598 and they were Indian structures."

"James compared that to his hometown of Oklahoma City first inhabited in 1889, six hundred years after the building of this church." There was significant damage to the front façade of the cathedral, but the towers were still standing and its five doors were still usable. The interior of the building had suffered some damage with most windows destroyed, but the inspiring feel of the old cathedral could not be denied. Debris piles were being gathered by men at work but could not hide the pock marks of shelling and rifle fire. Still the structure seemed sound and gave the feeling of grandeur and everlasting; no matter what happened to the building, it still remained standing.

It was late in the afternoon when the two men decided to head back to the house where the rest of the team had gathered to spend the night. As they were leaving the cathedral, an old parishioner approached the two men. The old man asked if he could be of assistance to which James answered in French, "No. We were just admiring the cathedral and the work you are doing to rebuild." "We were just leaving to join our group at the AuerGesellschaft plant." The old man then responded, "The plant manager is here and helping with the debris removal. Would you like to meet him?" James then responded, "Yes. We are trying to recover some vital material from the factory and he could help us with an inventory listing of the contents." The parishioner called to Phillip, who immediately dropped his shovel and approached the three men. As Philip approached, James introduced himself and Martinez then asked, "Were you the plant manager at the Auer-Gesellschaft plant when the Germans retreated?" Phillip responded that he had been the manager until they closed the facility and dismissed everyone and left the area. He had not been back to the plant since its closing but knew much of the inventory or where a listing of all materials was located. James then asked, "Would you please lead us to the materials inventory of the plant? We have located several barrels of material we need to defeat the Germans but there may be more." Phillip agreed and followed the two American soldiers to the plant. On the way to the plant, the three men stopped at the old house where the rest of the team was resting. After Martinez explained what had transpired at the cathedral and the meeting of Phillip, Blake wanted to attend the small group heading for the plant. As they neared the plant, the plant manager exclaimed remorse in the damage, "There is so much damage, but we should be able to access the manager's office for the materials inventory." "I can't believe the damage without causing a fire to destroy the rest of the plant."

Martinez was explaining the meeting of Phillip to Blake when James announced, "Phillip and I have located the listing of all materials in the plant and discovered some important items." Blake was very interested, but it was late in the afternoon and felt that the gathering of more product would be dangerous in the dark. "Let's wait until tomorrow morning when we can examine the plant and its contents more safely." Phillip was more than anxious to help the American soldiers since some of the Orleans citizens felt that he had been a German sympathizer by managing the plant while the Germans occupied the area. Some of the citizens had threatened to expose him to public ridicule but would change their minds by a show of support for the American soldiers. James then suggested, "Phillip should stay with us tonight for his protection then show us the plant tomorrow morning." Blake agreed and thanked Phillip with a hardy handshake and an offer to share what food they had. Phillip had a better idea, "Come with me to my home. I have some good wine and cheese." Phillip then led James, Brian, Martinez, and Blake to his home, where they "suffered" through a typical French dinner with great company and much wine. The menu consisted of mignonettes de cheotrenil poleis a l'aigre-doux, sweet and sour venison, salmon fume, and bitter chocolate marquise. The rest of the team's members would just have to enjoy their dinner of K-rations, dessert of C-rations, and the packs of "dark fluid" and bread that Andre and his wife had given them. Still a pretty good meal.

Everyone was up early, especially John and Dino, who were to catch a DC-3 military aircraft to Taggia, Italy, to meet with the Italian underground. Blake thanked the departing team members and suggested that they meet in Marseille in three days hopefully after Blake, Martinez, and the two physicists had found the seven carloads of uranium ore in Toulouse. Martinez was a victim of "cotton mouth" following the night with Phillip and his wine, but everyone else seemed to have fared better since they had stopped drinking earlier in the evening while Martinez continued to enjoy more wine. Everyone was anxious to follow Phillip into the plant to determine if more needed supplies or equipment could be found. Blake, Martinez, James, and Brian were led by Phillip to the plant. Phillip was quick to point to a stack of small boxes inside his old office. "Those are the new proximity fuses that the Germans had intended to use with the biological gasses." James was quick to point out, "Those fuses would allow the gasses to be dispersed at a higher altitude and effect a much larger area and disable many more soldiers."

Phillip was searching for something in the files in his desk drawer. "Here it is, the invoice showing the shipment of several parts from Siemens Electronics that were to be installed into a cyclotron in Strasbourg." "The order was sent to the attention of Dr. Weiscoulter, physicist at the University at Strasbourg." Blake was surprised by the new revelations and radioed Major Powers with the news. It was another of the leads that kept the Alsos teams busy rounding up the physicists, their laboratories, their equipment, and supplies needed for the Allies to build the "super bomb." Two more valuable and important findings in

Orleans and then the revelation of the cyclotron in Strasbourg and Dr. Weiscoulter.

Blake placed Phillip in protective custody of the four soldiers at the plant to be released following the demolition team's arrival and removal of the uranium, fuses, and proof of shipment of the cyclotron parts. Phillip was now a local hero by leading the American soldiers into the German plant and would not be harmed as a German sympathizer. Blake and the rest of the team thanked Phillip for his help and especially the wine and fantastic dinner and left Orleans in two jeeps headed to Toulouse. Major Powers ordered four soldiers to accompany Blake's team to Toulouse but Blake was in a hurry and did not wait for the reinforcements. They would have to make their way to Toulouse by themselves. They could contact the team by radio when they arrived in Toulouse.

John and Dino Meet Enzo and Nora

The DC-3 landed at the Taggia grass airfield midmorning. It was still not considered safe for American soldiers to be in the northern part of Italy. Although the Germans had retreated, there were still a few stragglers from the German Army along with Italian soldiers still supporting the Third Reich. The warring French underground had not been a problem in Italy, but they were close and John and Dino would have to search for the illusive uranium in areas under their control. The last sighting of the lost uranium ore had been the off-loading at the port of Marseille of the ship from Genoa with the new crew of German soldiers. Enzo and Nora of the Italian underground had been busy with other projects in Italy and had not followed the progress of the uranium ore once it left Marseille supposedly heading toward Arles. John and Dino were to coordinate their movements with Blake's team and they were to meet in Marseille in three days following their mission in Toulouse. John was anxious to start the search for the 1,400 tons of uranium ore moving north toward Arles and had proposed to Dino that they work with Enzo and Nora to track down the shipment. They could always return to Marseille to meet Blake's team in three days, but in the meantime, they could start their search. The reception at the airfield was cool. Nora looked wonderful. It was still a shock to John to see the leader of the underground to be such a beautiful woman. She was still upset that Enzo had exposed the underground to close scrutiny even though their mission was a resounding success in finding and apprehending the three physicists in Venice. John started the conversation with Nora, "I am really glad to see you again. Your help was deeply appreciated and I hope we can work closely with you again without causing friction between members of your group." Nora was hot but cooled at seeing John and the statement from John and she responded, "It's good to see you again also." "We look forward to working with you again and especially the chocolate and nylons along with the ammunition and medical supplies you provided to the local underground." John then asked, "Where is Enzo? We will need his help again to track the shipment of 'yellow dirt' to Arles." "We are needing to find the shipment and recover it for my country." "We do not want it to fall into the hands of the French, the Russians, or the Germans." "It is vital that we recover it to help win the war against the Vichy in southern France and the Third Reich." Nora explained, "We must be very careful during daylight hours. There are enemy operatives everywhere." "Enzo will meet you tonight at the small farmhouse we have established for your operations." "It is located close to the village of Le Muy across the French border and closer to Marseille." Nora had made arrangements for John and Dino to access the house and a car to get them there. She also had provided a road map to bypass the inspection station at the French border and a contact number for her and Enzo should they need more assistance. Radio contact would be possible when Enzo returns and would be preferable to telephone calls and much more private. Nora provided information to John on how to avoid detection for their team and especially the radio during their time in France.

The trip up the coast toward Marseille was really beautiful with several places where the road came close to the coast making the Mediterranean Sea visible. The beaches were vacant this time of year, still a little cool for even the hardiest swimmers. The road through Nice showed little damage from Allied bombing but Italian troops could be noted in some parts of the city. Beyond Nice, the road leads through Cannes and were not damaged and turned slightly north to Le Muy where the map that Enzo had drawn showed the way to a small nondescript rock house in the middle of town. John was hungry and tired after the flight from Orleans and the drive to Le Muy. "Let's find something to eat before dark. We should keep a low profile until hearing from Enzo." Dino did not argue but did suggest, "I could use a little wine too." Of course this part of the world had a long history of producing the finest wines to be found anywhere but John wanted a California wine. Dino then said, "Are you crazy? You want a 'foreign' wine?" "And from your home state?" "Maybe you should just ask for a glass of water." John was just playing with his friend and finally agreed to find some food and something to drink. As they were about to leave, another old car drove up to the front of the house. Enzo appeared at the front door earlier than expected and embraced both the Americans. "It is good to see you again. We have missed all the activity and trouble you two caused during your last trip here." John and Dino then grabbed the arm of Enzo and led him out the door in search of food.

Blake's Team in Toulouse

This was dangerous territory. Most of the Germans had either surrendered or had been pushed north and out of France but leaving pockets of Germans trying to stay alive and separated from their battle groups. The absence of the French Army and local police forces serving in the Army further north or in Germany created a perfect vacuum for lawlessness and anarchy to incubate and flourish. The French underground, common criminals, and lost German soldiers made the situation really dicey. Fighting broke out over the most insignificant reason and the combatants would change sides from time to time depending on the direction of the wind and temperature and how hungry they were. The only combatants fighting for their survival were the German soldiers just trying to get home. The underground and the criminals were fighting to rid the area of the Germans or for the right to a piece of ground or a building or a pretty girl. Fortunately for Blake and his team, there were many French underground members who were actually fighting for France and their villages. Oftentimes they would be the only police force and judge to provide justice for the masses of French citizens trying to recover from the ravages of war. Complicating the situation were Italian soldiers still aligned with the Germans before Mussolini was deposed and those that joined the allies to rid their country of Mussolini and the Germans. It was really difficult to determine if you had encountered a friend or more likely a foe. As they encountered the people in the area, it would be necessary to communicate in their languages; luckily James and Brian spoke both French and Italian while Martinez spoke French fluently.

Blake estimated that they were still two hundred-plus miles to their first stop on the way to Toulouse. The City of Clermont-Ferrand was west of Lyon and still considered the northern or central part of France. They would pass through the famous area where the Bourges ruled and the town of Vierzon both established during the Roman Empire along the Cher River. Normally a really beautiful country but currently trying to stay out of the war. There was little industry in the area and almost no strategic military targets. Bombing sorties and large military battles had destroyed very little of the area, but there were still areas of fighting and destruction, mainly by the French underground and lost German soldiers.

Blake noted that the war was different here. This was an unfamiliar war. You could trust no one, stay prepared to kill, or be killed and a war with no conscience. Blake knew he needed help working in this area and Major Powers had ordered several members of the French underground to assist, but Blake didn't know if they were to be trusted. It would be much safer to wait and work with the Italian underground that John and Dino had great success and trusted completely. That would take time, probably three or four days, time that Blake didn't have. The war was being won by the Allies but there were still many targets to find. There were uranium inventories, heavy water, and the scientists to be found to prevent the Third Reich from producing the first "super bomb." Then there was the possibility that the Russians could beat the Allies to the materials and build the bomb themselves. Even though Russia was an ally in the war against the Third Reich and Japan, they were considered to be the next enemy to freedom. The trip to Clermont-Ferrand was without incident, although many of the village people watching the American soldiers pass through their areas were not waving flags, throwing flowers, or singing welcoming songs. They were still not free to begin rebuilding or living their lives as they wished. The people just looked tired. Tired of the war, tired of the lack of electricity and water, tired of the lack of common items like buttons, sardines, and shoelaces. This part of France is still considered north or north central and not occupied immediately after the German invasion. Later in the war, much of the area was occupied by both German and Italian armies. That truce came to a halt when Mussolini was deposed and the northern Italian Army was liquidated by the German Army as the rest of Italy began to support the Allies in driving the Third Reich out of Italy, France, and eventually Germany. At one point in the German retreat, 750 Italian soldiers were executed by the Germans because they were considered enemies following the Italian government's decision to support the Allies.

Allies became enemies quickly in this war.

The team neared Clermont-Ferrand early afternoon and decided to take advantage of the daylight and continue south toward Toulouse. Blake had been studying a map of the area and decided to spend the night at Lempdes at the edge of the Auvergne mountains to avoid traveling after dark. The team had not encountered any trouble thus far but decided to not press their luck. They found a small hotel in the outskirts of town where they could conceal their jeeps in a small courtyard and away from inquisitive eyes, get some sleep, and possibly enjoy a little French food and wine. There was no food at the small hotel; that didn't stop Blake from a wishful menu choice. Blake asked Martinez, "I wonder if we could find some Southern fried chicken to take out?" Martinez was considering another menu item. "Probably not here, but I would rather have some beef tacos with a bottle of tequila." Blake responded, "I would go for that, but add some queso and chips and easy on the salt." James was listening to the conversation between Blake and Martinez in amusement then added, "Oh, I would rather dine on some fine K-rations followed by a dessert of our latest C-rations and a glass of filtered and stirred but not shaken ice cold Rocky Mountain water." Brian, in the meantime, had been writing a letter to his wife but had to add, "Not me. I'm going with Blake for some Southern fried chicken with bread pudding desert and a Coke." Everyone seemed to be pleased with their menu selections and was just waiting for a waiter to take their orders from their imaginary café. Blake finally became tired of the wait and suggested, "Let's try another restaurant. The service here is ever so slightly 'crappy,' so let's move." Brian pleaded for another five minutes to finish his letter to his wife before the four men left the small hotel in search of something to eat.

Really a beautiful old town, mostly two- and three-story buildings with red tiled roofs and narrow cobbled streets. The perfect setting for the invention of the 2CV, a creation of Paul Boulanger of the Citron Company. Built in Lempdes as economical transportation to replace the wheeled carts of the many farmers in the area and first called "An Umbrella on Wheels," or as some called it, "A Two-Horse Vehicle." Unfortunately, for the four men looking for something to eat, the town appeared deserted. As the men walked down the narrow streets, the scent of something cooking was detected by Blake. The rest of the party quickly stopped to determine the direction of the scents. No more laughter or light conversation; this was serious business. Find the source of the scents. Each of the men seemed to note the scents coming from a different direction, Blake and James pointing in two directions while Martinez and Brian pointed in two others. In the street with its high three-story walls, there were only two directions they could travel, either up the street or down where they had just entered. The two scientists were in heavy discussions concerning the detection capacity of the others' nasal orifices while Martinez began following his nose to a small alley just off the street. Martinez thought it was beef fajita he was smelling. Blake followed Martinez down the alley to the smells of what he thought was barbecue. The scientists were still trying to deduce who was the best "smeller" when Blake motioned them to follow him down the alley. Martinez found the source of the scents and smoke. He had entered a small covered patio in a walled garden, a world away from the world at war. He raised the lid of a dish to find "la cote a l'os limousine" while on the table next to the covered dish were several plates of "la braserade perigourdine." Martinez was interrupted by a loud high-pitched voice calling him things he did not recognize from his formal French training. He quickly recovered from the shock of the interruption by speaking more formal French and apologizing for his behavior. He explained that he had been drawn to the food by the wonderful aromas and that he and his friends were seeking a restaurant where they could find a great meal like the one she had prepared. The loud high-pitched voice finally softened to explain, "There are two small restaurants in the village, but they are closed by now. Are you soldiers?" Martinez answered by saying, "Yes, madam, we are American soldiers on our way to Toulouse but staying here tonight before we leave early tomorrow." "We are tired of the government-issued rations and looking for some authentic French cuisine." "I apologize for the interruption of your meal and our rude behavior. We will leave you and your family to dine uninterrupted." As Martinez turned to leave, he winked at Blake and motioned for the four men to leave but was again stopped by a softer high-pitched voice. "Please join me and my family for dinner. I have cooked more than enough. We welcome the American soldiers who have liberated our country from the Germans." Just as she had asked the four men to join her family for dinner, the rest of her family came out of the house. The small high-pitched voice belonged to a tiny woman in her seventies while her husband was even smaller and probably in his eighties. There were two grandchildren staying with the grandparents, ages eight and ten, while their father was a forced laborer in the factories in Germany and their mother was serving as a secretary to the Vichy government. Other family members were either fighting with the French Army in Germany or had joined the French underground to protect their village from the Germans and the Italians that still remained in France.

The meal was fantastic and the company was even better. Blake found it hard to understand how some people survive a war by compliance while others, even in the same family, fought hard to bring back the peace. Especially difficult to understand is the impact of war on the young and old. They just had to survive until the warring parties stopped shooting at each other and the innocents that happened to get in the way. The four men left the French home after many thanks and hugs and exchanging of good will. They had a great meal and now needed to prepare for the next day.

Everyone was up early. Brian was putting the finishing touches on the letter to his wife, James was packing, while Martinez and Blake were loading the jeeps to complete their trip to Toulouse. Brian asked James if he was married and why he did not write letters to anyone. James responded, "I had a wife once but she found someone she liked more and ran off to California with the guy." "It was not a pleasant marriage and I have tried to forget ole what's-her-name." That got a laugh out of Brian just as he was sealing his letter to his wife. "Sounds like you have already forgotten her." James then asked, "Were you asking about plaintiff number one or plaintiff number two?" That question got more laughter as Brian stuffed his finished letter into his jacket to be mailed.

Blake with Martinez interpreting approached their host for the evening to explain, "Thank you for the hospitality." "How much do we owe you for the comfortable evening's stay, wonderful shower, soft and clean bed, towels, and indoor plumbing?" The manager then explained, "There is no charge. You and your friends are the first soldiers to stay in my hotel since the Germans left the area." "I want to thank you for helping to liberate our village." Blake graciously accepted the hotel owner's generosity, shook his hand, stood at attention, and saluted the gentleman before leaving. He also left an envelope on his bed containing several thank-you notes from each of the team members along with 300 French francs.

The 160-mile trip to Toulouse was really a treat: some of the most beautiful in wonderful spring weather. The war had little effect on this part of France. Small- to medium-sized villages like St. Flour, Rodez, and Albi with no significant military value passed by comfortably while everyone stayed vigilant of possible dangerous contact with the remaining warring parties. The team decided to make their home base Saint-Sulpice, a suburb of Toulouse and parallel to the railroad tracks leading to Toulouse. Contact with Paris and Major Powers was made to secure the military team and several trucks to hopefully recover and move the uranium ore to Marseille. Blake felt confident they would find the uranium quickly and move on to Marseille. Major Powers had additional information about Dr. Werner Heisenberg. "He has left his laboratory for his home at Urfeld." "You must hurry to complete your Toulouse mission and proceed to Haigerloch, Hechingen, and Urfeld." "John and Dino will have to handle their assignment alone."

The French and Italian Underground

John and Dino were following Enzo through a maze of alleys and dark cobbled stone streets to a small sidewalk café that Enzo had known from previous visits. While Dino and Enzo were talking over a large glass of wine, John had something else on his mind. He couldn't get the thought of Nora out of his head. He had been hoping to spend more time with Nora. She was fascinating, beautiful, and yet led a large military-like underground operation that was the best ally the American Army had in northern Italy. She even made dark military fatigues look good. John could not imagine how or why such a creature could become involved and lead a secret and clandestine group as the Italian underground. He had to learn more about Nora and had spent several hours with Enzo and Dino before he felt he could broach the subject. He finally asked Enzo, "Can you tell me how Nora became involved with the underground?" Enzo was in the middle of a large bite of lasagna and did not respond quickly. "I don't think you want to know." "It is not a pleasant story except for the ending." "I will give you a summary but please don't ask more questions." "She had been taken by the SS from her family to work somewhere in Germany where she escaped from a forced labor camp building parts for German aircraft." "It took her two months to find her way back to Italy." "Both of her parents and one of her sisters had been killed by the German SS in her absence." "She found her ancestral home burned and a mere skeleton of its former self." "She found her other sister living in the burned house hiding in the dark and wet basement with no heat and little to eat." Her sister had been raped and left for dead living in the burned basement of their home." Her family had been suspected of conspiring against the German occupation of northern Italy following the deposition and death of Mussolini." Enzo took several more bites and a long drink of Italian wine before continuing. It was obvious that he was close to tears. "She and her sister came to my door late one night after avoiding several pro-German Italian soldiers and a regular German patrol." "Neither of the sisters had not eaten anything in over three days and were dehydrated and near exhaustion." "My family took them in and fed them just before they collapsed and slept for two days before regaining enough strength to talk." Enzo then stared me straight in the eyes and said, "The first thing she said was a pledge to rid the world of the evil Third Reich and to join my small group of partisans." "Her sister died several days later."

That was more than enough information John needed to know about Nora. A super-strong spirit forced upon her by her enemy. It was the reason John felt close to her and why he felt that she needed a friend, someone who could appreciate her without using or abusing her and someone she could trust.

John was picking at his food and lost his appetite. He did feel like drinking more. Enzo and Dino had finished their dinners and Enzo wanted to change the subject. "How do you want to proceed tomorrow to find the 'yellow dirt' in Arles?"

John was finally jolted back to reality and stopped thinking about Nora. "We may need the help of the French underground to follow the road and rail tracks to Arles to find a warehouse large enough to store such a large shipment." "We have the equipment to measure radioactivity to help locate the uranium ore." "It must have traveled by truck or train, but it is certain it was taken to Arles." "After the ore is processed in Arles there is the possibility it was transported to another processing plant in Nimes or Tarascon, both cities close to Arles." "The French underground could be very helpful in locating the shipment in either of those other cities while we concentrate on Arles." Enzo was considering the alternatives and added, "We can contact the French underground tonight after midnight." "I have a contact that is related to one of our underground members and should be easily found, but we must not divulge the nature of the material we seek or they may try to steal it from us." John and Dino were studying a map of the Arles area and marking industrial areas along the railroad and major highways. There were too many small- to medium-sized warehouses along the major roads while the larger warehouses were found east and north of town and located on the rails. One promising area of four warehouses was found east of town where three large warehouses were located on the west side of the tracks and one on the east side. The other more promising area was north of town. There were two complexes of several large warehouses located on the main tracks and two others on sidings off the main tracks. John then mentioned to Dino, "We must assume that wherever the uranium is stored, it will be guarded by German soldiers or French underground." "Probably the same soldiers that escorted the ship from Genoa to the port at Marseille." Dino then asked Enzo, "When you contact the French underground, ask them to check the four warehouses north of town and the two areas east of Arles while we check those on the east part of town." "Probably just check for German troop presence or at least German Army vehicles." John then mentioned, "We don't have much time and you need to stress the importance to get the information back to us quickly." "We need to locate the uranium and arrange to move it in two days to the port of Marseille." "We also need to contact Major Powers to have him send six five-ton trucks and military personnel to move the shipment when it is located before we meet with Blake's team on the third day." Enzo responded, "We will do our best to find the shipment by tomorrow night. You should be able to contact Major Powers tomorrow to arrange the pickup of the shipment." "You guys go to sleep while I handle the French underground." "In fact it's better that you don't meet them and therefore unable to identify them if the French underground or Germans capture and question you."

During the night, Enzo had contacted the French underground and asked them to check on the two sites west of Arles and the complex of warehouses north of town. That left the team with one target to eliminate as the location of the uranium ore, on the east side of town. Dino was studying the manifest they had obtained from Enzo's cousin in Genoa. The document mentioned that the final destination was the port of Marseille, but the German crew obviously changed the destination as the uranium was off-loaded at Marseille. Dino was about to discard the document in frustration when he noticed a note on the bottom of the manifest in German. Odd—the rest of the document was in Italian. Dino was curious and asked Enzo if anyone in his underground could read German. Enzo responded, "Of course, how do you think I know so much about their movements?" "I am very familiar with the language." "Why do you ask?"

Dino gave the manifest to Enzo and pointed to the bottom of the document and asked him to interpret for him. Probably nothing, but asked Enzo anyway. The notation read, "Several German words followed by T-214, E-549, U238 Belgium Co." Dino quickly picked up the map to check the number of the track leading north through Arles. "That's it, T-214 is track 214, a siding off the main track to the east part of town." "I recognize the U238 as uranium ore and the origin of the shipment was a Belgium company." "The E-549 I don't recognize." Enzo excitedly said, "It's probably the building number east of the tracks."

The team quickly moved to the siding on the east side of town. As the team approached the area of the four warehouses, the buildings had large numbers that were visible from the highway. The three on the west side of the siding were 546, 547, and 548. They could not see the number of the building on the east side of the siding due to large trees but assumed that must the 549 that they were seeking. As the team turned off the road and approached the building from another direction, the large number 549 appeared over one of the dock side doors. It was early in the morning but there were no vehicles or personnel visible from the parking lot in front of the building. Enzo then asked, "Do you think the building has been deserted?" John was quick to answer, "Not a chance. The Germans may have left the area, but the French underground would never leave it unoccupied." Dino then asked, "What should we do, wait for someone to open the building or what?" "Maybe we should wait for someone to open the office." Enzo then suggested that he walk around the perimeter of the building checking for open doors or personnel. Dino then responded, "Good idea, but be careful. You could be shot or arrested for trespassing." "We will wait at the front door for any sign of office personnel or warehouse workers." After about fifteen minutes, Enzo returned to find John and Dino waiting at the front door. Enzo then said, "Nothing."

At 0900 hours, a truck loaded with several workers and sacks of something approached the building. Enzo approached the truck and asked when the warehouse would open and when the manager would come to work. The truck driver responded in French, "I am the manager and I am coming to work right now." "What do you want?" Enzo responded in French and presented the manifest for the uranium shipment and asked if the shipment had been deposited in his warehouse. The manager responded, "I don't know. We have no inventory listing. The Germans did deposit many items here." "You can check for yourself if the items you are seeking are here, with a deposit." Enzo then asked, "A deposit?" "We just want to know if the item is here." The manager repeated, "A deposit will be required to enter the warehouse and if you find what you are looking for, that will be extra." Enzo then asked, "How much is the deposit for the three of us to check if our item is here?" The workers had left the truck and were moving the bags of something into the warehouse through the office door. The manager then noted that that John and Dino appeared to be Americans and rubbed his chin while calculating a figure for their entry. He finally decided, "100 francs per person and 100 francs for each item you take." John was listening to the negotiations and grudgingly gave the manager 300 francs for their entry.

There were no lights in the warehouse and the three flashlights searched the building slowly. John and Dino both carried a Geiger counter along with their flashlights in hope that the uranium would activate their equipment sooner than their flashlights. Several hours later, the three team members were hungry, tired, and frustrated. John had already asked to leave for some fresh air and to relieve himself. Dino and Enzo continued to search when suddenly Dino's Geiger counter went crazy. In the very back of the warehouse, there were stacks of barrels that had been marked as uranium ore but covered over with another marking of caustic soda and dangerous warnings along with the Belgium company's logo. As John returned, he was confronted with a stack of barrels from floor to ceiling on pallets. "There must be two hundred barrels there." Dino confirmed that the number was very close. We must contact Major Power immediately. "You better tell him to bring six large trucks and lots of French francs." "Be sure to tell him that the charge to take the barrels will be around 20,000 francs."

Seven Carloads of Uranium Ore, Toulouse

Martinez was up early checking their railroad maps. The team had decided to make Saint-Sulpice their base of operation while in Toulouse. The rest of the team apparently was going to sleep in. "Where is the coffee?" Blake asked. Martinez offered him a cup and poured some really dark stuff from an old ceramic pot found in the dilapidated barn they had chosen the night before that gave them a great view of the railroad tracks leading into Toulouse, but it was really uncomfortable lodging. Blake responded, "Wow, where did you get this stuff? It tastes like black house paint with a hint of asphalt." "Great isn't it!" Martinez interrupted the chastisement. Blake responded, "You aren't going to give that stuff to our two physicists, are you? They might not make it to the nearest latrine." "They are a little more gastrologically sophisticated than you 'wet backs' and us 'dumb gringos.'" "I still have some of that dark fluid that Andre Guston and his lovely little wife gave us for helping rebuild their bomb-damaged building that I can give to the physicists." "Maybe they will survive another day without having to drink your poisonous concoction." Martinez was not fazed by the obvious rebuke of his home-brewed coffee but just continued to enjoy his invention. Martinez finally decided, "Blake can find his own coffee from now on and fix it himself." "It is a little strong, but it did help him wake up in the morning." Breakfast was "wonderful" with K-rations and his dark concoction. Everyone finally was awake enough to continue their search for the elusive seven railcars.

They drove parallel to the tracks and as closely as possible watching for the railcars with the select numbers that would identify the cars containing the uranium. Unfortunately, there had been more numbers painted over some of the older numbers on the cars they passed and really slowed the process of elimination. As they passed one large warehouse with many railcars parked, they spotted one of the targeted railcars. The warehouse had no identification posted on the front as they parked their jeeps. It was still early, probably too early for most employees, and the team decided to avoid the front door and walk around to the back of the building where the railcars were parked. Blake was leading the team and was concentrating on the list of railcar numbers that contained the uranium ore when he was confronted by an armed Italian soldier. Blake's team stopped in their tracks and raised their arms over their heads. The soldier was alert and pointing his rifle at the midpoint between Blake's shoulders. Brian was quick to identify the team in Italian. "We are American soldiers. Do not shoot." "We are under orders from the allies to find seven railcars from Belgium." The soldier was not interested in who the intruders were or what they sought. He motioned with his rifle barrel to move the team to the back of the warehouse where several other soldiers were sitting on large crates enjoying a quick smoke before returning to their guard posts. An officer was in the group and quickly came to assist the guard with his new prisoners. The Italian officer finally asked, "What do want and why are you here?" More soldiers joined the officer and pointed their rifles at the team. Brian repeated his earlier response to the officer's request. "We are American soldiers ordered by the allies to find seven railcars from Belgium. We mean you no harm and ask that you help us find the railcars." Brian could not tell whether these Italian soldiers were still loyal to the Third Reich or not but decided to trust his instincts and assume that they were loyal to Italy and just recently an ally in the fight to remove the Germans from Italy and France. The team was still standing with their arms raised over their heads and growing anxious about their predicament. Brian took the initiative to show the officer their orders which were in Blake's breast pocket. The officer told Brian to keep his arms over his head as he approached Blake. Brian told Blake that he should stay still, leave his arms over his head, and let the officer reach into his breast pocket in search of their orders. Blake froze, completely still, and allowed the Italian officer to search his pockets for their orders. Blake was scared to death but couldn't help but thinking about a similar situation in the movies where someone was searching the inside of another's pockets just before he burst out laughing— it tickles. Fortunately for the team, Blake kept his composure while the Italian officer searched for their papers. It didn't take long and the officer withdrew the papers and began to read the orders.

Brian spoke again before the officer had finished reading their orders. "Let me read them for you. They are in English." The officer smiled and spoke in English. "Yes, I can read and even speak English, I attended Cambridge in 1932 through 1935."

The officer then ordered the soldiers to lower their weapons upon finding that the American soldiers were on a mission to retrieve some material shipped from Belgium.

Brian then described the single railcar that had been spotted as the team drove by the rail yard. The Italian officer did not have any of the records of shipments at his disposal and indicated that the rail master would arrive shortly and could identify every railcar in the yard. The Italian officer then directed Blake's team to relax. "I will discuss your situation with the rail master. He is part of the French underground and they have taken possession of the warehouse since the German Army's retreat." "Your orders may not convince the rail master that he should let you take any of his railcars." "You may need to barter with him because he thinks the warehouse is full of valuable treasure." "My orders are to make sure none of the military equipment housed here is not removed, and we are to shoot anyone attempting to enter the warehouse without authority."

Brian and the rest of the team had relaxed and just waiting for the rail master to arrive. Brian was concerned. "The Italian soldiers are guarding the warehouse that the French underground has claimed as their 'treasure.'" Brian went on to say, "The Germans have retreated and not a threat, but who will we negotiate with for our railcars, and what do we have that we can negotiate?" Blake finally mentioned, "I thought it was me that was confused." "The Italians are now allies in driving the Germans out of Italy and France. So are the French underground." "The French underground feels that they own the warehouse and the Italian soldiers are here to prevent any of its contents from disappearing." "In New Mexico we would call that a 'Mexican standoff' and not a safe place to be."

Two hours passed without the rail master. Finally a shiny black German staff car came roaring into the rail yard. The Italian officer, Blake, and Brian stood to meet the small gray-headed and white-bearded man as he exited the German staff car driven by another old gentleman, apparently also part of the French underground. The Italian officer introduced the rail master to Blake and Brian but did not try to ask permission to search his warehouse and rail yard, at least not yet. The rail master was no more than someone's great-grandfather who had assumed the position as directed by his fellow underground members. Probably ninety years old, portly, and wore frameless eyeglasses. As the German staff car drove off, the rail master motioned for the party to come into the warehouse where he maintained a small office. The rail master finally spoke, "What can I do for you?" Brian was still quiet while the Italian officer made small talk to lighten the tension in the room. He finally explained their need for some supplies to force the Germans out of France. The old man was anxious for the Germans to leave France but was still reluctant to share their "treasure" with the allies. Although the underground had no financial interest in its contents, their wartime bootie, or "treasure" as they called it, had much value to the returning government of France that was in exile in London awaiting the exit of the German forces. The French Army and the local police force hopefully would also be returning soon as the Germans retreat.

The Italian officer and Brian were trying to explain to the old man that they were looking for seven numbered carloads of uranium ore from Belgium when a secretary interrupted. The secretary explained, "The numbered railcars you seek are parked in the rail yard." "Two of the original nine railcars were moved further west and toward Bordeaux last month by the Germans." "The seven remaining railcars are located on track 16n about five hundred meters from the office." The old rail master finally added, "I will show you where they are located, but you will have to remove the contents. The railcars must remain here." Brian and the Italian officer could relax; the ore could be removed without having to barter for them.

The Italian officer, the rail master, and the Alsos team located the seven railcars just where the secretary said they would be. Unfortunately, the doors had been tampered with but the contents were intact except for one open barrel. Apparently no one wanted any of the small heavy barrels of uranium ore that appeared to be "yellow dirt."

Blake then asked the Italian officer if he would post a guard at the railcars to ensure that the uranium did not disappear during the night. "Yes, of course, we will watch the shipment tonight in hopes that you will be able to unload the contents by tomorrow." Blake assured the Italian officer that they would be able to move the shipment by midafternoon tomorrow. Blake now had the task of contacting Major Powers in Paris to arrange for several trucks to move the uranium to Marseille by tomorrow. He already had four armed soldiers coming from Paris to protect the team, but they still would need the trucks. Blake then asked James, "Would you contact Major Powers in Paris to have six five-ton trucks here by midafternoon tomorrow to transport the uranium we have found today?" James agreed and began searching for the elusive radio and decided to take a jeep some distance from their location before using the radio just in case someone was listening to the transmission and would try to triangulate its location to destroy it.

Major Powers was more than excited about finding the railcars of uranium. "We will have the six trucks there by midafternoon and move the uranium to Marseille." He continued, "Thank the team for me and tell them I will buy them a beer the next time I see them." "You will be leaving for Marseille as soon as the trucks arrive to join John and Dino." "You should beat them there by a full day." Major Powers then commented, "Take the day off. You have earned it."

Chapter 12

Major Powers's Mission

Major Powers was really pleased with the progress his teams had made. Blake's team had found the railcars in Toulouse and Nate's team had found two of the physicists on the list of "absolutely needed" along with their centrifuge and research material. John and Dino and their team had acquired three of the "absolutely needed" physicists and moved them to Tunis. Blake and Martinez had located and arranged for Dr. Curie and his cyclotron to be acquired and taken to London. So much success, but so much remained to be done. As the Allies drove the Germans out of occupied territories, they exposed more targets on the "absolutely needed" list. There had been no further contact with the Russian spies, at least to his knowledge. The Allies were winning the battle to acquire the "absolutely needed" list of assets and that worried Major Powers even more. It had been relatively easy to gather the "absolutely needed" assets to date and no injuries to any of the team members. The push toward Berlin and to eastern Germany would be much more difficult especially with the Russians pressing their advance toward Berlin from the east. It was feared that Dr. Heisenberg could be one of the last of the "absolutely needed" physicists on the list and Alsos intelligence had indicated that he had moved his laboratory to the Bavarian Alps and directly in the path of advancing Russian troops. To find and liberate Dr. Heisenberg would require that the Alsos teams would be working outside of the American Zone of Occupation and deep into the Russian and French zones of occupation as agreed upon at the Yalta Conference. They had even run into resistance in crossing into the French zone of occupation, and they were a staunch ally. Russian zone infiltration would be more difficult since Russia was considered the next "enemy" to freedom-loving democracies in Europe and throughout the world and had teams similar to the American Alsos teams in operation.

Major Powers had just received information of another target that had been discovered by Blake's team. Cyclotron parts were shipped to the University at Strasbourg and more of the proximity fuses along with more uranium oxide. There were too many targets and not enough recovery teams and he felt inclined to find the assets in Strasbourg himself. He had not been directly involved in any of the recoveries to date and really wanted to leave immediately for Strasbourg rather than sit in Paris and wait for the telephone to ring or be given a radio dispatch; he was especially tired of the mounds of paperwork necessary to document the various Alsos missions. His jeep was parked in front of the hotel just waiting for something to do, but before Major Powers could leave, he would need to arrange for two armed soldiers for security followed by two trucks to remove the uranium, cyclotron parts, and the proximity fuses. He realized that he did not need approval to go to Strasbourg, but he decided to contact the 12ᵗʰ Army headquarters to report his trip and the length of his stay away from Alsos headquarters. He got the customary response as he reported his trip to the headquarters office: "You're going where, for how long, and you expect to take two trucks and two armed soldiers to be taken off the battle lines to chase some scientific equipment?" Major Powers had heard of this type of exchange as several of the team leaders had reported similar responses from headquarters staff regarding needed equipment and supplies and personnel. He then remembered why Martinez was good at overcoming these types of roadblocks in gaining needed supplies: he "borrowed" them without permission. Of course the supply people didn't appreciate his "messing up their inventories" either. He finally received the supplies and equipment. He also found that "rank" had nothing to do with the response from supply personnel. They told everyone regardless of rank that they had better things to do and go bother someone else. Major Powers was obviously offended by the clerk's attitude, but what good could come from a confrontation and report of insubordination? Reporting the insubordination would only slow the pursuit of the cyclotron parts and uranium in Strasbourg. He got his two security personnel and two trucks and drivers and decided his mission was much more important than the retribution of the supply clerk. Major Powers understood that the supply clerk was under similar pressure as Major Powers and all soldiers in the war; *get it done* even if you had to step on a few toes in the process.

It was 4:30 in the afternoon and 190 miles to Strasbourg when the small convoy finally left Paris and would mean a probable overnight stop in Nancy. The road conditions and military actions would dictate the speed of the small convoy and he did not want to jeopardize the mission by excessive speed and carelessness. He did not want to approach the university in the dark and his intelligence concerning the exact location of the uranium and cyclotron parts was sketchy. It would take finding the exact location of the needed assets by trial and error or asking local residents.

The trip to Strasbourg took the small convoy through several towns and villages and the timing could not have been better. More convoys of Allied military equipment heading east toward the German border kept a good pace and they reached the outskirts of Nancy just as the sun was going down. As the small convoy approached Nancy, the military traffic continued directly through the city while Major Powers's team took a circuitous route around the southern part of the city seeking a place to pull off the road to spend the night. It was dark when the small convoy stopped at a crossroads that did not appear on their map. There was no traffic from any of the intersecting roads. It was totally dark on a cloudy and foggy night that hid the moon and eliminated any light. Their vehicle lights pierced the darkness and fog to expose the large cork oaks lining the roads and completely surrounded the small convoy. It was becoming difficult to find a place suitable for the vehicles to pull off the road to provide some shelter from the elements and to give the military vehicles some cover from other passing vehicles. The area had been recently liberated from German troops as the 3rd Army pushed the Germans toward the German border, but there had been warnings that small pockets of German troops or deserters still could be encountered. Major Powers was examining the road map on the hood of his jeep by the light of a flashlight held by one of the armed guards when a horse could be heard approaching. Major Powers responded, "Take cover and be prepared to fire on the horse."

Out of the fog came a young girl riding a beautiful chestnut-colored mare. The headlights of the vehicles and flashlights were exposing a young girl near exhaustion and crying as she approached. She appeared confused as she approached the American troops. She had expected the soldiers to be

French troops that had liberated Strasbourg on November 23. Major Powers motioned for the young girl to stop and helped her down from her mount. He did not speak French but Corporal Vance, one of the security soldiers, addressed the girl in French, "Are you okay?" "What is wrong?" "Let us help you. We mean you no harm." Major Powers helped the girl sit in one of the jeeps and gave her his canteen of water and a chocolate bar. The tears continued but between sobbing and crying the young girl was able to explain her situation. "I ran from my home and took a neighbor's horse to find help." More sobbing. "My family is being held captive by some German soldiers that invaded our farmhouse earlier this evening." "I was in the barn gathering eggs when I heard the shots, I think three." "My mother ran out the back of the house screaming and motioned for me to run." "The soldier chasing my mother did not see her motioning for me to leave the barn as I ran toward our neighbors." "I heard another shot but did not look back to see what had happened. I just kept running." Major Powers then asked, "Do you know how many soldiers are in your house?" The girl responded, "No, but I heard more than one voice coming from the house as I ran." "My father is disabled from the First World War and I have two brothers and an older sister in the house besides my mother who ran out the back door." "I have to find help for my family. Will you give me a ride into the city?" Corporal Vance, interpreting for Major Powers, then added his plea, "We need to help this girl free her family from the Germans." Major Powers responded, "You're right, but we are not armed sufficiently to take on a party of German soldiers." "We need some Thompson submachine guns, concussion grenades, and a way to get the soldiers out of the house." The weapons the two security personnel carried were two M1 rifles and two .45 caliber semiautomatic Colt pistols. The drivers of the two trucks both carried M1 rifles and Major Powers had the standard officer's .45 caliber semiautomatic Colt pistol. Major Powers then responded, "We don't know how many soldiers are involved, their weapons, or their intentions with the family." "Ask the girl how far their farm is from here and if we can drive our trucks close without alerting the German soldiers." The young girl replied, "Our farm is about three kilometers from here and it is located about one kilometer off the road deep in the woods. Your trucks would not be heard from the road, but the lights might be seen from the house." Major Powers then suggested to Corporal Vance, "What do you think about our moving the trucks closer to the house but take the jeep closer to the house and leave the trucks off the road to keep the noise down?" Corporal Vance agreed with the plan as far as it went but then asked, "What do you plan to do after we get closer to the house?" One of the truck drivers then volunteered, "I know we need more intelligence before we can plan any action, but we are not totally without some offensive weapons." "We can make several Molotov cocktails and we have three flares in each truck if we need to add some light to the house." Corporal Vance then asked the girl, "Is there anything in the barn we could use as a weapon?" The girl answered, "Just a tractor, some farm equipment, two cows, and some chickens." Corporal Vance then suggested, "That would be a good place for us to stay and to get close enough to learn what the soldiers are planning." "We may find more weapons there also." Major Powers then responded, "If we had the exact location of the house we could radio for help and some strategic shelling, but it would be too dangerous without exact location coordinates." "Time is our 'enemy' too. We need to do something soon to prevent more shootings." Major Powers then asked the team if they agreed with the plan to move closer in the vehicles, leave the trucks off the road further from the house, and follow the girl back to her house and take refuge in the barn. More information is needed before we can do anything, but the barn would be a good vantage point to learn more of the soldier's intentions. The rest of the team agreed with the plan and Corporal Vance then told the girl of their plans to help her and her family.

The team made their way to the barn with the assistance of the young girl. Quietly, they crept through the undergrowth and grass to the rear of the barn. The interior of the dark barn was lighted by a single flashlight and contained several shovels, pitchforks, and hoes that could be used as weapons, but none of the team relished fighting with a shovel against a German Luger pistol or rifle. Corporal Vance had crawled closer to the house to determine how many soldiers were involved and what weapons they had and whether her family was restrained in any way. The rest of the team began searching the barn for anything that could be used as a weapon. The young girl said she could drive the tractor if needed and gave Major Powers an idea. "Can we use some of the tractor implements to protect the driver from rifle fire or some metal of some kind?" The young girl then said that many times she had maneuvered the tractor from behind the seat while plowing and would be out of the line of fire, but steering would be a problem. By this time Corporal Vance returned and reported, "There are three German soldiers that appear to be deserters and are armed with rifles only." "All family members are gathered in one room including your mother and their hands are now tied." "The soldiers were eating something that either your mother had prepared or they had found on their own and did not appear to be threatening any of your family." "The shots fired must have been warning shots since none of your family appears injured." "The soldiers are eating like they have not eaten for several days and I heard them asking for wine while one of your brothers retrieved from some place down stairs."

Major Powers then asked, "Is there a way we can get into the downstairs area from outside?" "If so, we may be able to get close to the soldiers without starting a war where someone could be shot. The young girl answered, "Yes, there is a way into the basement from the outside." "It is where we keep our canned vegetables, fruits, and wine."

Corporal Vance motioned for Major Powers and the other soldiers to confer at the front door of the barn. "It will be dangerous, but the young girl could return to the house with the eggs and appear not to be aware of the German soldiers." "She could volunteer to get more wine and bring one of the German soldiers with her to help carry the bottles." "We could be positioned in the basement to quietly take the soldier down to the ground and kill him if necessary." "The girl could return upstairs carrying several bottles of wine and explain that the soldier remained in the basement to drink more wine." "That would leave two solders that have relaxed and not pointing their weapons at the family." One of the drivers could fire one of the flares and fire his weapon from the road to distract the two remaining soldiers while we approach them from the stairs." "We could then tell them to surrender that they are covered or shoot them if they resist." "The girl will be the catalyst to make the plan work." Major Powers and the rest of the team agreed that the plan was workable but would mean that the young girl would be placed in danger. Major Powers then asked, "Does anyone have a better idea?"

Corporal Vance explained the teams plan to the young girl who had been sitting sobbing and wondering what would become of her family. "We have a plan that may free your family from the soldiers but we will need your help." The girl responded, "Anything. I only want my family safe." The girl agreed with the plan although reluctantly. She was scared that she might be injured but her fear for her personal well-being was secondary to the fear that something could happen to her family. Major Powers's team was getting into position before the girl entered the back of the house. One of the truck drivers had secured two flares to light the area and he was positioned close to the road armed with his M1 rifle and a Molotov cocktail. He was prepared to provide a diversion while Major Powers and Corporal Vance entered the house from the basement to capture one of the German soldiers as he descended the stairwell. Major Powers and Corporal Vance had made their way into the basement while the two security guards followed the girl as she approached the house. The guards stayed outside the house and out of sight. She had prepared an armful of eggs and several bottles of fresh milk to be dropped in her surprise to see the three German soldiers. As she entered the back door she called out, "Mother, help me with these eggs before I drop them." She had turned the corner into the kitchen and her back was turned while putting down the eggs as one of the German soldiers heard her and approached her in the kitchen. She was still calling for her mother when she turned to find the German soldier standing in the doorway. She screamed and dropped one bottle of fresh milk before the soldier could say anything. Finally, just as surprised as the girl, the soldier told her in French that they intended no harm to her or her family. "We are lost, hungry, and tired of fighting a losing war." "Your family is safe but tied to keep them quiet." The girl then responded, "Take what you need. If you need more I can show you to our basement." "We have fruit, vegetables, and wine in storage." The German soldier placed his rifle against the wall and then stooped to help the girl clean the floor of the broken glass milk bottle. As he was rising to dispose of some of the glass, he turned to find Major Powers and Corporal Vance holding weapons directed at his eyes and testicles. Corporal Vance had overheard the German soldier explain their situation to the girl and then explained, "You and the other two soldiers should surrender to us before the Russians capture you." "You will be imprisoned until the war ends, but you will be well treated, fed, and live with many of your countrymen." "The Russians will be in the area soon and they are looking for German soldiers to torture and kill in reprisal for murdering many of their comrades and private citizens." Corporal Vance continued, "Now tell your two friends to drop their weapons and place their hands on their heads." By this time, the guards at the back door entered to help with capturing the German soldiers. It appeared that the situation had been stabilized and the German soldiers would surrender as had the one in the kitchen. Suddenly, the truck driver on the road fired his flares and shot his weapon into the air in the planned diversionary move. The two German soldiers in the front of the house, unaware of the capture of their other member jumped into action and began shooting their weapons in the direction of the flares without seeing a target. It wasn't supposed to happen that way. The German soldiers were supposed to quietly surrender as they should have thought they were been attacked. Just as quickly, Major Powers and Corporal Vance fired shots into the bodies of the two German soldiers while their backs were still turned. Major Powers and Corporal Vance stopped firing and both men were horrified by the German soldier's reaction to the flare. They were just seconds from being told to drop their weapons and surrender but the flare and shots fired from the road changed all that. From being alive and spending the rest of the war as a military prisoner of war to sudden death. The third German soldier in the kitchen kept his hands on his head and remained still as he was still covered by the guards that entered the house from the back. Corporal Vance then ran to the two German soldiers on the floor in the front room to determine whether they were dead or wounded. He found them unresponsive, shook his head, and turned to Major Powers to acknowledge their death before turning to release the family from their bindings. He was speaking in French to the family, "You are safe now and your daughter is in the kitchen unharmed." "We are American soldiers on our way to Strasbourg and had stopped at the crossroads where your daughter found us." "She is a very brave young lady and you should be proud that she helped with your safety and release." "We will take the remaining prisoner with us to be imprisoned in Paris."

The family was finally released from their bindings when the father spoke, "We are very glad you saved us from the German soldiers. We did not know what to expect from them and we feared they had killed our daughter." Major Powers then spoke through Corporal Vance, "We are sorry that the German soldiers had to be shot, but it could have been one of us or your family." "We will move the bodies out of your house and hopefully you will not be bothered by more German deserters." "We can't spend the time to bury their bodies but maybe you can arrange to have them buried." It was now the turn for the mother to speak. "Thank you and your men for saving our family." "Life must go on." "You will stay for dinner so we can thank you." Without waiting for a response, the mother then pointed to her two sons and ordered, "You boys help the soldiers move the bodies and get some firewood and fetch some chickens." She then ordered her daughter to bring up some fruit, vegetables, and wine. It now appeared that the team would be treated to a meal and could spend the night here instead of hiding off the road in the woods. The two guards left the house to find the truck driver that had fired the flares and shots into the air as a diversion. They called his name and used their flashlights searching the underbrush for the driver. When the driver did not respond, the two guards called for Major Powers and Corporal Vance to help in the search. He was finally found beside one of the trucks with a hole in his helmet just above his left ear. The shots from the German soldiers were wild and at no particular target, just shooting wildly to balance the shots fired at them in a defensive move but had the desired effect. Corporal Vance thought to himself, *War is not fair or discriminating between the good and the bad. Everyone is bad.* The team now had four members.

The University at Strasbourg

One of the guards would have to drive one of the trucks to Strasbourg. Major Powers was now alone in the lead jeep while both guards were driving one truck and the other truck was driven by the assigned driver. The team decided to rejoin the large convoys of military vehicles moving toward Strasbourg rather than attempt to take the roads less traveled. The probability of meeting more German deserters was high while traveling less-traveled roads. On the main roads, many of the trucks and tankers moved slowly through the open country but drove much faster and closer to each other, almost bumper to bumper, to navigate a small village or town to avoid the possible saboteur. Much like the famous "Red-Ball Express," "Highballing to Victory," trying to keep forward units supplied with fuel and ammunition and something to eat. The truck driver in the team was familiar with this procedure but Corporal Vance, driving the second truck, was scared to death and was learning by the "seat of his pants," and just trying to keep them clean. On November 23, 1944, the city of Strasbourg was liberated by the 2nd French Armored Division under General Leclerc. Between the German invasion of Poland on the September 1, 1939, and the Anglo-French declaration of war against the German Third Reich on September 3, 1939, the entire city of 120,000 people was evacuated. For ten months the city was vacant until the arrival of the Wehrmacht troops in June 1940. In the meantime, the Strasbourg University was moved to Clermont-Ferrand, approximately 225 miles southwest of Strasbourg. The university remained in Clermont-Ferrand until May 1945 when it reoccupied the Strasbourg campus. Many Strasbourg residents were forced to fight with German soldiers on the Eastern Front against the Russians. These young men and women were called Malgre-nous. Many escaped to join the French resistance. Many of them could not leave the German Army to protect their families from being placed in forced concentration camps. The threat of being placed in concentration camps forced most of them to remain in the German Army fighting on the Eastern Front. The few

Malgrenous that survived the battles against the Russians on the Eastern Front were accused of being traitors by their French countrymen. In July 1944, 1,500 of the Malgre-nous were released from Russian captivity and sent to Algiers where they joined the free French forces to fight the Germans.

Following the liberation of Strasbourg by the French forces, the American 3rd Army Group had cleared the German resistance in Strasbourg and made it safe for Major Powers to approach the University of Strasbourg. He stayed in contact with the Strasbourg T-Force Command, a unit of the 1st Army, for assistance in gaining access to the university. Corporal Vance volunteered, "We should proceed by ourselves. The T-Force personnel will just be in the way and slow us down." "We can leave the captured German soldier with them to arrest and detain." Major Powers responded, "Okay, but we must be on our toes, there are still a few German soldiers trying to find their way home." "At some point we will need the T-Force if we move on to Heidelberg." On November 25, Major Powers took over the laboratories of the University of Strasbourg and all targeted equipment and seven physicists and chemists. One of the laboratory workers volunteered, "There are four of the scientists involved with nuclear research hiding in the hospital." Major Powers and Vance located the local hospital and found four of the physicists disguised as hospital personnel. Vance was thinking to himself, *I hope their patients were healthy and not needing surgery. Not a good place to get sick. Physicists would probably dissect the patients just to see what made them tick.* Here it was also proven that the Kaiser Wilhelm Laboratories headed by Dr. Werner Heisenberg had been moved to Hechingen, south of Germany. It was also learned that Dr. Bothe, another prominent German nuclear physicist had acquired the only working cyclotron in Germany and had moved it sixty miles from Strasbourg to Heidelberg. Vance could see more humor in the German's activity. "Another piece of heavy equipment not used and moved frequently just to hide from the Allies." Major Powers took Vance's advice about the Strasbourg T-Force Command. He arranged to have the T-Force Command intern the equipment and personnel at the university and hospital, leaving Major Powers and his team to concentrate on capturing the cyclotron in Heidelberg. Major Powers was concerned that he had asked his team to do too much. "Should we proceed to Heidelberg to capture the cyclotron or head back to Paris?" "The equipment is a vital piece of equipment used in particle acceleration." "It is the process used to smash particles together to change the particles and develop materials." "At least that's what I have been told." Corporal Vance was quick to answer. "I really don't know what a cyclotron is or what it does, but if it will end this war any sooner, I say we pick it up." The other members of the team were quick to respond in the affirmative. Major Powers then responded, "It may be dangerous and we will have to travel without the T-Force since they will be deployed elsewhere." "We may need a small T-Force to follow us due to the German stragglers still in the area and to help in moving the very heavy cyclotron." Again, the rest of the team agreed and decided to leave Strasbourg as soon as possible, without a small T-Force for support. Major Powers failed to tell the team what he had learned in Strasbourg of possible contact with a Russian team much like the Alsos team, intent on capturing the same nuclear scientists and assets.

Approach to Heidelberg, the Russian Teams

The Russian team responded to the radio contact from the "Mechanic." "The American Alsos team will be in Heidelberg just ahead of you." The "Mechanic" had learned from his contact within the American Alsos headquarters and had passed the information onto the two Russian teams heading to the city of Hamburg. The "Mechanic" continued, "The cyclotron located at the physics laboratory of Dr. Walther Berthe in the Kaiser Wilhelm Institute for Medical Research is a secondary target since the cyclotron is not a vital part of the assembly of the super bomb." "It is an important research particle accelerator, but we should concentrate on the vital pieces needed for our 'super bomb' production." "However, the American Alsos team may be in the process of removing the cyclotron for their use and therefore a target for elimination."

"I have been told that the team of four American soldiers is led by a major and they are not under the protection of one of the T-Forces."

The team leader of team two then quickly responded, "French tanks, trucks, and soldiers are everywhere." The "Mechanic" then responded, "You must avoid their contact by moving west of the city." "It will be dark soon and you can move into the city from the west along with the French Army and approach the Kaiser Wilhelm Institute late this evening to either eliminate the American Alsos team or if you beat them there, you could create a booby-trap for the American Alsos team as they try to remove the cyclotron." The team leader responded, "Yes, sir, but we must be quick and continue the trip to Hamburg." "We will possibly encounter Italian troops and French underground as they try to free the Vichy government that has been imprisoned nearby at Sigmaringen." "If we encounter American troops they most likely will be the American Alsos team headed to Heidelberg or returning to Paris."

The Kaiser Wilhelm Institute: Heidelberg

Major Powers was tired. He thought he really had no reason to be tired with all the time he had in Paris doing nothing but paperwork while the various American Alsos teams were doing all the work. He was still tired. He guessed the three hours of sleep he had on the hard floor of the fiveton truck last evening could be responsible, or maybe it was the constant reminder that he had shot two German soldiers and captured a third. The three German deserters had captured a farm family near Nancy, France, and his team had the chance to liberate them from the three soldiers, but two of the deserters were shot during the liberation. Then again it could be the tension involved in staying alert to German deserters heading home and trying to end their part in the war. He finally became aware of the real reason for being tired: he was just tired of the war and wanted to go home to his family for a little peace and quiet, just like the three German deserters.

"Operation Hanover, over." The radio jolted Major Powers awake from his day-dreaming. He reached for his radio to respond, "Operation Hanover, what can I do for you? Over." The reception was not crystal clear, but he could make out the simple warning, "Watch your back, you have company headed to Heidelberg, over." "Confirmed, over and out." It was the warning that he had expected but had never been exposed to and its implications. It meant that the Russians were present. This was the first contact with the Russian Alsos teams in his experience.

Apparently both the Russian and American Alsos teams were approaching Heidelberg for the same reason: the cyclotron at the Kaiser Wilhelm Institute and the laboratory of the famous physicist Dr. Walther Berthe.

Major Powers gathered his team to explain the situation to them. "We have been alerted that there is a Russian Alsos team headed to the same laboratory that we had targeted." "This is the first contact with one of the Russian teams much like our American Alsos teams." "They will be targeting the cyclotron and laboratory of Dr. Berthe for the same reason we had targeted Dr. Berthe." "The cyclotron is not a necessary instrument in the construction of the 'super bomb,' but Dr. Berthe is one of the foremost physicists in the world that would be a very important asset in building the bomb." "It's imperative that we reach the Kaiser Wilhelm Institute before the Russians to keep the famous physicist out of the hands of the Russians." "We need to move quickly and reach the institute as soon as possible." "I want Corporal Vance to accompany me in the lead jeep along with his M1 rifle and any other firearms that can be spared from the two trucks." "We must be ready for them as we approach the University." Corporal Vance then asked, "How will we recognize them?" Major Powers answered, "There are Italian, French, and a few British troops involved in the move east toward Berlin." Major Powers then explained, "The Russians are not supposed to be in this area. This occupational zone is in the French occupational area but being shared with the Americans and British." "The

Italians are in the area on their way to release their imprisoned Vichy government." "The Russians will not be in uniform in this area." "Stay alert to any civilians, especially traveling in a group or traveling with heavy equipment." "Trucks would be necessary to transport the cyclotron and the other laboratory equipment." "I'm sure the Russians will be trying to take advantage of the confusion of the various troops in the area." "We must get to the institute before the Russians to find Dr. Berthe." "Since we are in a hurry, Vance and I will enter the city alone in the jeep to move quickly, find Dr. Berthe, and leave as soon as possible." "The cyclotron is too heavy to move quickly and we will have to destroy it or if possible leave it in the custody of the Allied forces." "Vance and I will meet you here just before sundown, if all goes well." "We will stay in radio contact with you should we need your help."

As Major Powers and Corporal Vance approached the institute, it became obvious that the Russian Alsos team had not been there. There were French and Italian troops occupying the entry into the building where Dr. Berthe's laboratory was reported to be. Major Powers introduced himself to Dr. Berthe and asked him to accompany him and Corporal Vance to Paris. Dr. Berthe acted as if he was expecting to be contacted and agreed to accompany them to Paris after he had some time to collect his papers and luggage which had been previously packed and stacked in his office. Dr. Berthe then mentioned that the famed chemist Richard Kuhn was in the laboratory and should also be taken to Paris. Dr. Berthe volunteered to show Major Powers the cyclotron and proceeded to escort the two men into his laboratory. As important as a cyclotron is in particle acceleration, this one was really small compared to the twenty or so Major Powers had seen in the United States. Apparently this cyclotron was one of two in operating condition in Germany while others were apparently planned or under construction. Major Powers was introduced to another physicist in the laboratory by the name of Lanard. He had been a loyal Nazi since 1918 and had received the Nobel Prize in 1905. His value to the Allies was questionable not due to his age but his belligerent attitude toward modern physics. Major Powers decided to let him stay in the laboratory as the Allied armies were making the area safe and he could be used to restart the physics program at the institute. Major Powers decided to leave Dr. Berthe and Dr. Kuhn in the custody of American intelligence that entered the area recently. They would be safer in their custody and would make the trip back to Paris much easier.

It had taken a little longer than planned for Major Powers and Corporal Vance to leave Heidelberg. Corporal Vance then radioed ahead to the two trucks waiting the return of Major Powers and Corporal Vance. "Operation Hanover, over." The radio shook the three soldiers waiting in the two trucks. They responded, "Operation Hanover, what is your status? Over." Corporal Vance then responded, "Our ETA is thirty minutes. We will proceed to Paris." "Over and out."

The Russians Hear the Conversation

Matrei had overheard the radio communication and ordered his team to be on alert. Matrei radioed the "Mechanic" that they had come into contact with the American Alsos team and asked for orders to proceed. The "Mechanic" responded, "You must work fast, if the American Alsos team leader is approaching their two trucks to return to Paris, they probably have Drs. Bothe and Kuhn in custody and proceeding to Paris to transport him out of the country." The "Mechanic" then ordered Matrei to have his team attack the two trucks parked along the road to Heidelberg and if possible take a hostage to be interrogated.

Matrei went into a quick conference with the two teams and deployed half of the teams to cover the two vehicles from either side of the road while the other half approached from the rear where one of the American Alsos team members had just climbed into the rear of the transport. Within seconds, the two occupants of the front of the first truck were shot before they could respond. The third team member in the back of the truck then called Major Powers to report the attack.

"Operation Hanover, over." Corporal Vance then answered the radio call, "Operation Hanover, what's up, over." "We are under attack, we are under attack, I repeat, we are under attack!" Corporal Vance then responded, "Who is attacking you and can you secure your position? We are within twenty minutes of your position." The radio responded, "I don't know. They are civilians. Look like farmers!" Corporal Vance then implored the caller, "Hang in there, we will be there soon."

The Russian attack was fast and furious. The three soldiers in the trucks had no chance under such heavy fire. Two of the soldiers were shot while the third was taken into custody for interrogation. The "Mechanic" then responded, "Take the American trucks, the radio, and the driver." "We may need him and the equipment in other missions." Matrei then asked, "Don't we want to attack the two soldiers approaching from Heidelberg?" "No, we should leave before they arrive. We don't want to be implicated in this attack." "We are supposed to be part of the Allied forces."

Major Powers Arrives Too Late

Corporal Vance exclaimed, "Where are the trucks?" The trucks were gone but there were two bodies lying in the road where the trucks had been parked. "Who would have ambushed our team and taken the trucks?" The only thing to do now was to load the two bodies into the jeep and head back to Paris. Major Powers was the first to admit, "We should have been more careful and taken a T-Force with us." "The trucks are gone and one of the drivers is missing." "It must have been the work of the French underground. Farmers would not be so well armed or likely to fire on American soldiers." Corporal Vance then reported, "The truck's tracks showed that they were driven north toward Hamburg." "We should report that the vehicles were stolen and a driver taken hostage." Major Powers then responded, "Let's get out of here. You can report it to headquarters while I drive."

Chapter 13

Hechingen and Haigerloch

"The Russians are approaching Hechingen and Haigerloch," Blake explained to Nate. "We must drive to Urfeld, where it is reported that Dr. Heisenberg has moved to his home rather than stay with his laboratory and nuclear pile." "The Russians are after the nuclear pile and uranium that we must find before we can leave for Urfeld." "We will take Martinez and a small T-Force team along with two large trucks first to Hechingen to find the nuclear pile and uranium then on to Haigerloch for the laboratories of Drs. Haan and Dievner and more supplies." "The trucks should return quickly to Paris while you and I take a jeep to find Dr. Heisenberg at Urfeld." Nate, who was becoming really bored with all the details and orders, then interrupted Blake, "Whoa, take a breath." "I know we have a lot to do in a short period of time." "Let me take Davis in a jeep and find Dr. Heisenberg while you and

Martinez take the rest of the Army to find the nuclear pile and laboratories in Hechingen and Haigerloch." "I know timing is important and especially with the Russians also approaching the two villages." "Heisenberg is our most important target." "While the other targets are important, I don't want to have to fight the Russians for the stuff in the two villages." Blake had shown his frustrations with all the details of the missions and Nate made perfect sense—not like him at all. Blake then said, "Okay, you win, but get your butt in gear." Nate continued to try to consolidate and to end the instructions, "Besides, Urfeld is closer to Paris and will be quicker to recover Heisenberg." "You and Martinez would have to backtrack to pick up Heisenberg in Urfeld."

As Blake and Martinez led the small T-Force team and approached Haigerloch, there was sporadic small-arms fire causing his team to retreat to the outskirts of the village for the evening. At dawn the next day, the team entered the village unopposed. Shortly after entering the village, a German general approached the team showing signs of surrender. One of the T-Force team members spoke German and could interpret for Blake. The general wanted to surrender his force of one thousand soldiers. Blake was shocked. He didn't have any idea about how to take one thousand troops into custody. Blake then asked the general to wait until the next morning to surrender his troops because his general was too busy now but could be available in the morning. The German general then left to return the next morning. Blake frantically radioed Major Powers in Paris. "What are we going to do with a general and one thousand troops who want to surrender tomorrow morning here at Haigerloch?"

Major Powers was shocked too. He reasoned that the general wanted to surrender to the Americans rather than be captured and sent to concentration camps by the Russians. "We will have a senior officer and a large T-Force there by 0900 hours in the morning." "In the meantime, try to get your work done rather than search for prisoners." Blake then returned to the encampment where his team was to spend the second evening. Martinez was amazed at the events of the day. He had never seen a German general and couldn't believe he wanted to surrender his one thousand troops. He finally reminded Blake of the work to be done tomorrow. "Once we get rid of the German troops, how do you want to proceed to the laboratory?" "Is the exponential pile located in a cave here in Haigerloch?" "Why was it moved from Berlin?" "Was it due to the bombing in Berlin or was it because Heisenberg wanted to be closer to his home?" Blake finally interrupted Martinez, "Enough with the questions. Go find the cave." "It can't be too hard to find." "It is located at the bottom of a cliff face and a large castle is located above the cliff face." "Take a guard or two and find the cave before dark, we need to start moving the pile and supplies as soon as possible." "The Russians are approaching from the east and we must beat them to the cave."

Martinez and one guard from the T-Force left the encampment just in time to see another German commander approach Blake with another white flag of surrender. This commander had only seven hundred troops to surrender. Blake had to tell the commander the same story that he told the general earlier in the afternoon. The American general was too busy and would be able to accept his surrender tomorrow morning. Blake now had 1,700 German troops that were to surrender tomorrow morning. Instead of waiting for the senior officer and the large T-Force from Paris to arrive, Blake ordered his team, including the small T-Force, to find the cave at Haigerloch and begin evacuation of the laboratory. He couldn't imagine staying at his encampment to receive the 1,700 German troops; he would leave that exciting experience to Major Powers and the T-Force coming from Paris.

Martinez had located the cave but had bad news. The cave entrance had been blocked by a large pile of rock probably from a dynamite charge from above the cave entrance in the cliff. Martinez radioed Blake the location of the cave, "It is exactly where you said it would be." "In the face of a cliff and below a castle." It was late in the afternoon as the team assembled at the cave entrance and began to remove the rocks from the entrance, rock by rock. The team finally stopped moving rocks well after dark when Blake said, "That's enough for today, and we can start early tomorrow morning to complete the excavation."

The next morning Blake received some grim information from Paris. The Russians were making rapid progress to Haigerloch and should arrive by midafternoon. Blake then decided that he could not waste time moving the rocks one at a time and ordered Martinez to blow the rocks away from the cave entrance with several pounds of dynamite. Before Martinez found the dynamite to excavate the cave entrance Blake had another assignment for him. "Can you drive a French tank?" "I saw an abandoned French tank about a mile from the bridge over the Eyach River, a feeder to the Elbe River." "It would have to be crossed by the Russians as they approach Haigerloch from the east." Martinez then replied, "Is the Pope Catholic?" "Where is the tank and I will move it to the bridge if it is in operating condition." Martinez then took one of the big trucks with some diesel cans to find the tank. Blake and Martinez found the tank very close to where Blake had described. The tank appeared to be in good shape with no damage noted. He then mounted the turret to examine the interior. Although Martinez spoke French, there were no instructions on its operation. The tank had been stripped of its radio, ammunition, and shells and would be useless in battle. The small French tank was a Char B1 with a four-cylinder Renault engine that runs on diesel. Blake had found two extra jerricans of diesel and had emptied both cans into the fuel tank. Blake then banged on the side of the tank. "Can you drive this thing or not?" "What's holding you up?" Martinez then replied, "You dumb 'Gringo,' you scared the hell out of me." "Everything seems to work, the batteries are charged, the lights work, but the gas tank was empty." Blake banged on the side of the tank again and told Martinez he had just put ten gallons of diesel in the tank. Martinez felt comfortable with the tank's operation and tried to start the engine. With a little urging, the engine came to life with a belch of black smoke. Martinez was moving the transmission around trying to find neutral gear when his foot slipped off the clutch. The little tank jumped into action in reverse. Before he could stop the tank it had crushed the two empty gas cans and pushed the big truck into a huge tree, crumpling the right fender and breaking the headlight. Blake was the first to respond. "So, I guess the Pope is not Catholic." "I thought you said you could drive this thing." Martinez was unfazed and responded, "I didn't say I was a good driver." "At least we now know where reverse gear is." "Out of my way, artist at work." "I'll see you at the cave after I park the tank on the bridge."

Martinez had finished his first assigned task and was preparing the explosives to clear the rock from the entrance to the cave. He approached the team moving rock from the cave entrance.

"What's holding you up?" "Can't you get into the cave?" Blake was impatient. "Hurry up, we need to find and move the nuclear pile and laboratory before the Russians get here." Blake finally heard the warning from Martinez. "Fire in the hole!" Martinez yelled to alert every one of the impending explosion.

The Explosion

The "Mechanic" responded to the sound as his team approached Haigerloch. "What was that blast? Was it in Haigerloch?" "The Americans have blown the entrance to the cave and the laboratory of Drs. Dievner and Haun." He then asked, "How far is the cave?" The team leader responded, "Probably five miles." "There is a column of French soldiers approaching from the south, probably heading to free the remaining Vichy government imprisoned at Sigmaringen." "We must wait until the French column passes before we try to find the bridge over the river Eyach." "The Americans were ordered to stay clear of the French and Russian zones of occupation by the Yalta agreement, but here they are." "They obviously have beaten us to the cave, but we have the advantage now of beating them to Hechingen." The "Mechanic" then ordered the team leader to send two men to the cave at Haigerloch to recover anything of value that the American Alsos team had missed. The "Mechanic" and the rest of the team were to proceed to Hechingen as soon as possible to beat the American Alsos team to the laboratory of several prominent scientists and physicists. Klaus had learned from his contact in American Alsos headquarters that the British had found a vicar in London that had been born and raised in Hechingen and had described the buildings where the laboratory would be located. He described the building as a large spinning mill with a basement. It contained a textile factory, a brewery, and an electric plant. Perfect location for a nuclear research laboratory.

The two-man team responsible to find and take anything of value that the American Alsos team had missed in their haste to leave Haigerloch were approaching the Eyach River and noticed a French tank had been parked on the bridge to eliminate any traffic over the bridge. The two men moved on foot around the tank and arrived just in time to see the last of the American Alsos vehicles disappear heading to Hechingen. The cave entrance had been blown clear of rocks, but the Americans had left a reminder that they had been there. It was a large white piece of fabric covering the opening to the cave with the drawing of a fence with the top of a ball-headed man with a huge nose looking over the fence with the fingers of both hands appearing over the top of the fence. Under the drawing of the figure was the phrase written in English—"Kilroy Was Here"—in broad black letters which the two soldiers could not read.

The two soldiers entered the cave vary cautiously. They suspected that the American Alsos team had possibly planted booby traps or mines and were staying close to the walls of the cave as they entered. From the lights of their miner's helmets, they came upon a large hole in the ground, probably where the exponential pile had been located. Obviously missing was most of the uranium metal blocks and carbon blocks. However, in their haste to leave the cave they missed several small piles of uranium and carbon blocks. The two Russian soldiers found little else and moved the uranium and carbon quickly to their truck on the other side of the bridge over the river. Within two hours, the two soldiers were heading toward Hechingen to meet the "Mechanic" and the rest of the Russian team.

The "Mechanic" was furious. After learning that the American Alsos team had taken most of the assets at the Haigerloch cave and especially furious that they had left a reminder that they had beat the Russians to the cave. This was his first encounter with the phrase and picture but had been told by others of the presence of the phrase used by the Americans. "Kilroy Was Here" would remain in his memory forever as a reminder of the competitive nature of the American Alsos teams. The two men that had been left at Haigerloch did have a little good news. They had found several stacks of uranium metal and carbon blocks. They had also uncovered several containers of heavy water left behind by the retreating American Alsos team. The

American Alsos team had also beat his team to Hechingen and taken into custody several prominent physicists and chemists but left quickly to avoid contact with the Russians.

Chapter 14

The War Is Over

Nate was headed for Urfled with two armed guards. Unusual for an Alsos team where more scientists and guards and often times several T-Force Command personnel would be involved. His goal was to find and "encourage" Dr. Werner Heisenberg to join him and his guards to accompany them to Paris to be interred with other German physicists until the war was over. Dr. Heisenberg was the recognized leader of most of the work leading to the development of the atomic bomb for Germany. He had been the chief physicist in the Kaiser Wilhelm Institute for Physics in Berlin before the bombing of many of the facilities of the institute. To conceal much of their work and hopefully avoid Allied bombing, he and several other physicists established their laboratories in the south of Germany in the general location of Haigerloch and Hechingen. Much of their work there had been either underground or concealed in various facilities as a spinning mill, a brewery, an electric generating plant, and a school. As the French and Russian forces neared the facilities at the two laboratory locations, Dr. Heisenberg left his laboratories and bicycled the one hundred miles to his home in Urfeld to await the Allied forces. It was obvious he did not want to surrender to the Russians.

Nate and the two guards neared Urfled late in the afternoon to locate Dr. Heisenberg. As they found him, he was packed and ready to leave but wanted to spend the last night with his family before departing the following morning. The next morning, Nate and the guards apprehended Heisenberg and then traveled first to Heidelberg to join the other interred physicists. Unfortunately, the facilities were not comfortable for the physicists and they were moved to Versailles. Once again, the facilities were inadequate and uncomfortable. Eventually the ten physicists were moved to Farm Hall, England. The Allies did not want these scientists to fall into the hands of the Russians and retained them at Farm Hall for approximately six months. Following the war, the scientists were released and moved back into Germany to begin the rebuilding of the sciences in Germany.

Nate and Blake were back in Paris following their missions to Urfeld, Haigerloch, and Hechingen. Drs. Otto Smitt and Reginald Graff of Nate's team were also in Paris awaiting for another mission or to be released from the service. Sergeants

Martinez, Davis, and Cornwell were also at their favorite outdoor café enjoying the peace and quiet. Major Powers and Corporal Vance had returned the previous week and had completed their report on the attack of their team on the road leading to Heidelberg. They still had not learned what happened to the two trucks or the captured truck driver. Major Powers suspected they were Russians in civilian clothing, but there was no proof to substantiate his suspicions or to point to another group involved in the killing of the two team members and taking of the two trucks. It was reported by the Russians as they captured Berlin that Hitler and his new wife had committed suicide on April 30, 1945. The following week, most of the German troops surrendered. At last, Germany and most of Europe and Africa were finally free from the Third Reich.

The scene in Paris was jubilant. General Charles de Gaulle had returned from exile in London to reestablish the French government. The Vichy government had been rescued from Germany and was being integrated back into the French government, with the exception of the Nazi sympathizers.

Nate and Blake had joined Sergeants Martinez, Davis, and Cornwell seated at their favorite outdoor café admiring the spring weather and pretty girls on their bicycles. Nate was curious what would each of the team members planned for the future. Martinez started by saying he was to be released soon from the Army and planned to join a friend of his driving big rigs in Texas and New Mexico. Blake couldn't help but tell him to get a "bunch" of insurance—he drove his tank into the water at Normandy and crashed another into a truck and completely destroyed two gas cans when he couldn't handle the clutch in the small French tank. "Okay, okay, I'll just drive trucks with automatic transmissions." The "roast" was on! It was

Martinez's turn to remind Blake about the "dark fluid" of Andre's and his falling off his stool and giggling uncontrollably at French jokes he didn't understand. "You don't even remember where you slept that night." Nate then reminded Blake of his beautiful Hawaiian shirt that smelled terrible after rummaging through the trash in Corpus Christi. Then Blake said, "You didn't smell too good either." "And you are such a tough guy that an old man had to save your butt while trying to quiet a German soldier." Martinez now lashed out at the two physicists trying to find the food they smelled in the street. "There were only two directions we could proceed to find the food, but you guys argued about who was the better smeller." "Lucky you had me to find it for you, or you might have starved to death."

Major Powers was now Colonel Powers and had to intervene to hold the merriment to a dull roar. "Dinner is on me again tonight." "Don't make any plans to party too much, we will be flown to London early tomorrow morning to complete the

Alsos missions and to be discharged." "Those of you in the military will receive your new orders to be redeployed." "See you at 1800 hours tonight."

Epilogue

The Second World War in Europe ended in early May 1945 with the capture of Berlin and the surrender of all German forces. Adolf Hitler and his new wife had committed suicide on April 30, 1945, but the German forces did not surrender until May 6 and 8 with some services and submarines surrendering as late as May 14. The various Alsos missions were a complete success. The missions were responsible for gathering much of the raw material, equipment, and several of the physicists and other scientists that helped the United States develop and deploy the first atomic bomb and develop nuclear energy.

Nate and Blake were released from the Army and returned to civilian life in Magdalena and Socorro, New Mexico. The two journalists had no job at the *Mountain Mail* since it had closed. Nate rejoined his friend Brandon, the past editor of the *Mountain Mail* at the Hamburger Palace they had opened in Magdalena. Both men worked in the hamburger café and continued their writing about ghost towns and old mining communities in the nearby Black Range and Gila Wilderness. Blake joined his wife in their specialty curios shop in Socorro to design and sell unique turquoise jewelry. Nate was happy to be driving his little '32 Chevy truck that the FBI had left for him while Blake was still driving his scrappy little pea green '41 Ford Coupe. Nate, Blake, and Brandon meet occasionally at the Water Canyon Lodge to reminisce about the dawning of the Atomic Age and to attend the annual trip to Ground Zero in the desert south of Socorro where it all began. Nate and Blake did have the chance to record the Alsos missions but no longer wanted to pursue writing for any paper. They just retired from journalism.

Dr. Otto Smitt returned to his chemistry class at New Mexico Institute of Mining and Technology College. He and his family were finally free of the issues that brought him to New Mexico; the Third Reich had been defeated and no longer existed. He still calls his friend Dr. Reginald Graff who had sponsored his move from Germany and it was Graff who had insisted that he become involved with the Alsos missions to help rid the world of the Third Reich. They both regretted not being more involved in the development of the first atomic bomb but recognized the importance of the Alsos missions to provide many of the necessary assets to develop and deploy the first atomic bomb.

Major Powers continued his career in the Army and finally promoted to full colonel. As the assigned leader of the Alsos missions, he helped defuse the German and Russian attempts to develop the first atomic bomb. He meets occasionally with his retired commanding general just to reminisce and continue to marvel at how much was accomplished by the Alsos missions.

Sergeant Martinez left the Army following his term of commitment and returned to El Paso, Texas. He continued his education at Texas Western College and graduated with honors in European languages. He bought into a trucking firm and helps drive big trucks throughout Texas and New Mexico. His buddies from the Alsos missions, Sergeants Davis and Cornwell, rarely communicate, but when they do, they try to top each other's lies as they did in Paris during the war. Theirs was a different war from their counterparts. They never fired a shot during the Alsos missions and never missed a meal although the quality was often questionable. Always had a place to sleep but sometimes not the most comfortable setting. They each had one thousand ways to prepare K-rations and C-rations to make them palatable.

John Anello rejoined the FBI and was stationed in San Francisco where he could see his best friend Dino Tanaka occasionally. Dino had moved from Los Angeles where his mother was still selling flowers in her small gift and flower shop. Dino was now the managing editor of the paper in Sacramento, California.

Their meetings somehow always ended with conversation regarding the Italian underground and the Alsos missions. Neither man had returned to Italy but both men never forgot the people they met and the work within the underground. John especially had not forgotten Nora. He wanted to get to know her better but the opportunity never materialized. John had learned from Enzo that Nora had gone into politics after the war and was representing the people of Genoa and the surrounding villages. She was already a great leader in the underground before leading the people of Genoa after the war.

Writer's Notes

As the United States entered the war in Europe, it was believed that the Germans were close to developing the atomic bomb that would serve to propel the Third Reich to world domination. The Alsos missions helped defuse the German program and eventually slowed the building of the Russian atomic bomb.

The term "atomgeddon" was coined by the author to help describe the controversy in building the bomb. Many of the developers of the "gadget" were against the bomb. It was believed by many that the explosion of such a device would consume the world's atmosphere while others objected to the destructive power of the bomb. Instead of a bomb destroying a building, the atomic bomb could conceivably destroy a city. War using nuclear weapons would change the definition of war. Instead of injury between warring armies, nuclear war would destroy masses of warring parties and civilians alike. Everyone would be involved in the battles. There were also those that feared the unknown and the unexplainable. There would be no winners or losers; everyone would be a loser.

It has been seventy years since that first test in the desert south of my hometown of Socorro, New Mexico, on July 16, 1945. Controversy still exists concerning the development of the first atomic bomb. "Fat Man and Little Boy" began the dawning of the atomic age. Small in comparison with today's weapons but powerful enough to end the Second World War. It took complete destruction of two Japanese cities by those two bombs to convince the combatants that nuclear war was not worth fighting. Since Hiroshima and Nagasaki, a nuclear weapon has not been used in war. However, the dawning of the "atomic age" also created the "cold war." It took Russia four years to test their first atomic bomb following the ending of the Second World War in 1949. Since then, the countries that have developed nuclear weapons have multiplied and the cold war continues to grow and has become a warm if not a hot war. War with atomic weapons becomes "atomgeddon."

Since writing my first book, *Countdown to Atomgeddon: The Race to Build the First Atomic Bomb*, I have been asked repeatedly why I wrote the book. I have answered the question several ways including the following: a fanatic interest in the subject, my older brothers prodding to write about the subject, inspiration to write because of the visit to the National Nuclear Museum, and of course, the most common answer, I had nothing better to do with my time in retirement. The main reason I have written the book was that when thinking about the dawning of the atomic age at the age of five, I had slept through it while most people who witnessed the explosion were affected dramatically. Probably the most important period of time in modern times and I slept through it. I still cannot believe I slept through such a momentous occurrence. In April 2014, I visited the National Nuclear Museum in Albuquerque with my wife and my brother and his wife. It occurred to me that I had lived through most of the time and events represented in the museum but had forgotten most of the details and almost all of the people and places involved. I then reasoned if I had forgotten the details, probably many others had forgotten also. Plus the fact that as I discuss my book with young people, few have any recollection or interest in reliving the period. The first book and this one should serve to remind us of the significance of the developments since the "test" on July 16, 1945. It ended the Second World War, it created nuclear energy and nuclear medicine, and it has created the cold war. War without battles but always preparing for war. A defensive war with no end in sight. War that is so devastating that no one would dare start a nuclear war for fear of instant and total reprisal. War that produces no winner, just all losers.

This is the second book by James Howell concerning the "race to build the first atomic bomb." As the United States entered the war in Europe, it was determined that the Germans were very close to developing an atomic weapon. It was one of the major reasons that President Roosevelt determined that it was in the best interest of the United States and the rest of non-Axis countries of the world to stop the Third Reich and Japan from dominating the world with such a weapon. To help slow or stop the Third Reich from developing and deploying the first atomic bomb, a group of American soldiers and scientists were brought together to form teams of "scavengers" to find and confiscate materials, scientists, atomic research, and laboratory equipment necessary for the development of the German "atomic engine." These teams were to follow the advancing Allied armies as they pushed the Germans out of occupied areas of Italy, France, Belgium, and eventually, Germany. The teams were to gather the needed assets and ship them back to the United States or Great Britain to assist in the building of the nuclear weapon in the United States. These teams of scientists and soldiers were made part of the "Alsos missions."

James Howell's first book dealt with the test bomb in the desert of southern New Mexico while this book deals with much of the activity to build the weapon and to acquire the needed assets from Germany before they could develop their own weapon. Many of the scientists and especially the physicists emigrated from Germany before and during the war as part of the Third Reich's program to eliminate the Jews from Europe. Many of these scientists became part of the Manhattan Project. Many other scientists stayed in Germany but were hampered in building the weapon by Allied bombing and ground forces. Germany's resources were directed toward other priorities while the Alsos teams captured many of the resources and physicists.

At the end of the war, ten physicists were returned to Germany from imprisonment in England to rebuild the sciences in Germany. None were forced to immigrate to the United States. Although the first bomb test was tested successfully in the desert south of Socorro, New Mexico, most Americans knew nothing of such a weapon. That was July 16, 1945. The rest of the world knew about the weapon on August 3 as the first of two nuclear weapons were dropped on Hiroshima followed by Nagasaki to end the Second World War.

References

1. Goudsmit, Samuel S., *Alsos*, API American Institute of Physics, 1996, 219–222.

2. Goudsmit, Samuel S., *Alsos*, API American Institute of Physics, 1996, 215–217.

3. Goudsmit, Samuel S., *Alsos*, API American Institute of Physics, 1996, 102.